KINGDOM AWAKE
PRODUCTIONS

Born Again as Kings

The end of satan

And the beginning of God's Kings!

And one of the elders says to me, Do not weep. Behold, the lion which [is] of the tribe of Judah, the root of David, has overcome [so as] to open the book, and its seven seals. And I saw in the midst of the throne and of the four living creatures, and in the midst of the elders, a Lamb standing, as slain, having seven horns and seven eyes, which are the seven Spirits of God [which are] sent into all the earth: and it came and took [it] out of the right hand of him that sat upon the throne. And when it took the book, the four living creatures and the twenty-four elders fell before the Lamb, having each a harp and golden bowls full of incenses, which are the prayers of the saints.

And they sing a new song, saying, Thou art worthy to take the book, and to open its seals; because thou hast been slain, and hast redeemed to God, by thy blood, out of every tribe, and tongue, and people, and nation, and made them to our God kings and priests; and they shall reign over the earth.

Revelation 5:5-10

Presented To:

_____

From:

_____

Year:

_____

"Born Again as Kings" Copyright© 2022

by Cory D. Gray All Rights Reserved

All rights reserved. No portion of this book may be reproduced in any form without permission from the publisher, except as permitted by U.S. copyright law. ***For permissions, ex. printing out copies for ministry purposes contact:*** *Kingdombiz@protonmail.com*

This title is also available at https://bornagainaskings.com

You can also visit our main website with more resources at https://kingdombusinesslifestyle.com

---

Second Edition 2023 – by Kingdom Awake Communications

Published in the United States Of America

ISBN: 979-8-9865963-0-3 (Paperback)

John 16:11 "...of judgment, because the ruler of this world is judged."

Table of Contents:

Ch.1 What Does Kingdom Mean?

Ch.2 Reconciled Back To The Garden

Ch.3 The Only End Times Left Is When All Of Heaven Invades Earth

Ch.4 Understanding The Blessing & The Promise of Abraham

Ch.5 Understanding The Kingdom Takeover Message

Ch.6 Jesus Has All Authority In Heaven and Earth

Ch.7 Now That We Know The Message, Let's Make An Impact!!

"Born Again as Kings"
CH.1 WHAT DOES KINGDOM MEAN?

God, we just thank you for the time to be here together in the name of Jesus around your Word, around your Truth, and with you Holy Spirit. Holy Spirit guide us. Help me release these realities, these truths in an easy way that we can all understand and see so clearly. The Kingdom is like this little mustard seed, that grows into the largest of all garden trees. Father let this seed of your Kingdom grow in our hearts, and in our lives, in Jesus name Amen.

Alright, so the first topic we're going to be talking about is, "What is the Kingdom?" What does Kingdom mean? This is so important. I have been teaching this message about the Kingdom for 10 years now at the time of writing this book. This is the message God gave me while I was locked away in a prison cell with no one to turn to but Him.

One day I had a lady speak to me, and she said, "Cory, the reason why people are having a hard time understanding the Kingdom message is because they don't actually know what the Kingdom is or what it means." We have all these catch phrases about Kingdom: building the Kingdom, living in the Kingdom, working in the Kingdom, but what are we actually talking about?

When I first started reading my Bible and searching out the meaning of "Kingdom," I read the part where Jesus says, "do not worry" "put first the Kingdom of God, and all these things will be given." At that time I had a lot of problems, a lot to worry about, or so I thought.

I was just out of prison, knowing I was born again and trying to figure out how to follow God by myself. I didn't have anybody coaching me except for the Holy Spirit, which turned out to my great benefit. But, I had to figure out what that verse meant, "put first the Kingdom and all these things will be given." I had a real hard time at first with that scripture.

So this is what I did. I took out my Bible and an old school giant Strong's Greek Concordance, which I had purchased at a garage sale for like a dollar: the best dollar I have ever spent. I recommend every student of the Word get one, as well as an Interlinear Bible. Then I decided I would research everywhere in the Bible that said, "Kingdom." I literally took a note-book and hand wrote every single scripture that had to do with Kingdom. I wanted to write them on my heart and get them to renew my mind.

Then I looked at the Greek, looked at the Hebrew, looked at all the different translations and interpretations of Kingdom. I would write them on my marker-board and sit and meditate on these scriptures for hours.

After about 30 days of notes spread everywhere, and me sitting on the floor with them, I found out what Kingdom means! I remember one day I was like, "Oh, my gosh, Kingdom means Dominion!!! O my gosh, Kingdom means Dominion!! Oh my gosh!!"

This then left me with another task of understanding the Bible through the concept of "do not worry, but put first the Dominion of God, and all these things will be given." DOMINION, like what Adam had in the beginning!!! Many things started to connect together and make more sense. I am honored to share with you what I learned!

So when Jesus said, "Repent the Kingdom of God is at hand." He wasn't talking about a place and He wasn't talking about a feeling. He was talking about the Dominion of God which is now here on the earth to be restored back its rightful owners, God's

Children. This Dominion was what Adam was supposed to live with and utilize in all of God's creation. He was to multiply, be fruitful, and extend this blessing and dominion to the ends of the earth.

Genesis 1:26-27 Then God said, "Let us make man in our image, after our likeness. And let them **have dominion over the fish of the sea and over the birds of the heavens and over the livestock <u>and over all the earth</u>** and over every creeping thing that creeps on the earth." So God created man in his own image, in the image of God He created them male and female He created them.

Genesis 1:28-30 <u>**And God blessed them.**</u> **And God said to them, "Be fruitful and multiply and fill the earth and subdue it** and have dominion over the fish of the sea and over the birds of the heavens and over every living thing that moves on the earth." And God said, "Behold, I have given you every plant yielding seed that is on the face of all the earth, and every tree with seed in its fruit. You shall have them for food.

Adam had Dominion "over all of the earth", but as we know that serpent the devil came in and tricked him, causing him to divert this Kingdom / Dominion / Kingly Ruler-ship satan's direction by submitting to his will rather than the will of his Creator. That is what happened in the garden. Adam lost his ability to use God given righteous Dominion, also known as Ruler-ship or Kingship. The Hebrew word for this is "Radah."

God created the earth, He created the animals, He created the trees, He created everything. Then He put Adam and Eve in the garden to work the earth, to manage the earth and to be in command by using this Ruler-ship or Kingdom "over all the earth."

Unfortunately, they lost this ability to use Dominion. Instead of Adam and Eve having dominion over creation, creation began to have dominion over them.

Side note: I put the name satan in all lowercase because I see his name as the name beneath all names, and that he shall soon be wiped from the earth and even the minds of the future Kingdom Leaders, our children! In the future he will be remembered no more.

> Genesis 3:17-19 And to Adam He said, "Because you have listened to the voice of your wife and have eaten of the tree of which I commanded you 'You shall not eat of it,' cursed is the ground because of you; in pain you shall eat of it all the days of

your life thorns and thistles it shall bring forth for you; and you shall eat the plants of the field. **By the sweat of your face you shall eat bread, till you return to the ground, for out of it you were taken; for you are dust, and to dust you shall return."**

Adam and Eve went from blessed in the garden, to now stressed in the field. Living the life of toil, rather than receiving the divine provision of heaven. Rather than having Dominion over all the earth, the earth was dominating them. God even set up a Cherubim with a flaming sword flashing back and forth to make sure that man didn't enter in again and eat of the Tree of Life and live forever.

Let's pause. Let me stir up a question in you real quick...

Is it possible that the reconciliation of God through Christ allows us back into this "Garden" the place of abundance, Kingship, Ruler-ship, and Divine Provision of Heaven?? Is it possible that we can now enter past the Cherubim and eat of the Tree of Life!?

We're going to talk about this as well as how we can activate and release the "Blessing" and "Kingdom" in our lives in a future chapter. These are mighty faith filled Words spoken in the beginning over Adam and Eve (mankind). Adam and Eve lost the ability to fully manifest "The Blessing" and "The Dominion." These empowering words God spoke over them.

If you are in Christ, I speak these words over you today by the power of the Holy Spirit. "Be Blessed and have Dominion." These are very special words. We must understand the meaning of these words and how to apply them in our lives!!

We now know that the word "dominion" in Hebrew is the word "radah," which is the same word as kingdom; meaning to rule and reign. So, kingdom and dominion are used in Hebrew as interchangeable. I am excited to prove this to you and help you to rise into a higher level with God and to be seated at His right hand of authority with Christ Jesus!!

Now follow with me here closely. There is the Kingdom of God, which is the Dominion of God given to mankind to rule over earth. BUT then there's also the **"Message of the Kingdom,"** which is HOW the Dominion of God, working through His Children, empowers us to take back control and possess the earth. It is the STORY of God. Or in other words, the prophecy of how God's children with His Dominion, take back control from the evil one. This is called the **"Message of the Kingdom."**

Please get this; there is "The Kingdom of God" and then there is the "Message of The Kingdom of God."

> 1 Corinthians 4:20 For the kingdom of God does not consist in talk but in power.

The Kingdom of God is the power and the message about the Kingdom is how God's people use this power (dominion) to take over this world. This will all make sense shortly if things are not already clicking! Stay with me.

> Matthew 13:19 The seed that fell on the footpath represents those who hear **the message about the Kingdom** and don't understand it. Then the evil one comes and snatches away the seed that was planted in their hearts.

Now this is so simple if you think about it. In the beginning Adam had Dominion. He didn't actually lose it, because mankind still possessed it. He just lost his ability to use it because sin entered into his heart. This Word was still spoken over mankind. They never lost it, and I'll prove that to you later. But he lost his ability to use it because he yielded this Dominion to the wrong spirit. God's Kingdom or Dominion only functions through righteousness. Righteousness is the ebb and flow of heaven. Sin short circuits the Blessing and the Dominion. It also produces harmful effects and frequencies sent into God's creation. This is why the earth began to reject Adam's work and bring forth thorn bushes rather than fruit.

We must recognize that there's also this **"Message of the Kingdom"** the story that is woven all throughout the Bible about God getting his people back into positioning of Dominion, and back into positioning of Kingship. We constantly read in Proverbs and Psalms about there being a day the wicked will be no more and you will look for them and they will all be gone. Eventually, as Heaven continues to invade earth, all will be righteous, all will know God and everyone will be filled with His Spirit!!!!!

Hebrews 8:10-13 For this is the covenant that I will make with the house of Israel after those days, declares the Lord: **I will put my laws into their minds, and write them on their hearts, and I will be their God, and they shall be my people. And they shall not teach, each one his neighbor and each one his**

brother, saying, 'Know the Lord,' for they shall all know me, from the least of them to the greatest. For I will be merciful toward their iniquities, and I will remember their sins no more." In speaking of a new covenant, he makes the first one obsolete. And what is becoming obsolete and growing old is ready to vanish away.

The one called satan was not made for this earth. We have to finish him off and his name and the remembrance of him shall fade away as well. Jesus came to destroy the works of the devil, but we (the Church) have the glory of enforcing the **guilty** sentence pronounced upon him!!

Alright let's go to the book of Mark,

Mark 1:14-15 Now after John was arrested, Jesus came into Galilee, proclaiming the gospel of God, and saying, **"The time is fulfilled, and the kingdom of God is at hand; repent and believe in the gospel."**

We always hear about the repent part of this verse. We hear the preachers say that it means change your way, change your mind. And everybody's talking about that. However, that is not the fullness of the point of this scripture. Repent, *because* the

Kingdom is here. These people were sitting under darkness, but now a light had come, Jesus was the light that came to the people sitting in darkness. And that "Repent" means change your way of thinking and change your direction; yes, **because God's Dominion and God's Kingdom is now here!**

This meant that the people were not trapped under the dominion of darkness anymore. This was the time they were waiting for from the declarations and teachings of the Prophets who had come before them. Many students of the Prophets of that earlier time had a better understanding of Kingdom than most do in the 21st century. But all that is changing now!

What happened next? Jesus appointed his disciples and He sent them out to proclaim the Good News of the Kingdom of God. That it is at hand and it's here. Moreover, they cast out devils to prove that a superior Kingdom, a superior Dominion is now here on planet earth!! If that doesn't get you excited I don't know what will.

A truly superior Kingdom is here, and these disciples went out and they proved it! They didn't have to muster it up, they didn't have to try and pray in tongues and fast or anything like that. They just went out, cast out devils, laid hands on this sick, even raised dead people, because of this Kingdom / Dominion of God that was now flowing through them.

They had Kingdom operating in their lives. We have Kingdom operating in our lives. And there's a lot to say about the power of Kingdom. Kingdom is power. It is raw divine power. The power to reign as Kings on the earth. God spoke it over Adam and Eve. So that Word was on them, but they couldn't manifest it. However, some of us in Christ are leaving the life of toil to live the life of power, peace, joy, righteousness, abundance, Dominion, and Blessing in the name of the Lord Jesus!

Next, let's go to the book of Luke,

Luke 10:1-9 After this the Lord appointed seventy-two others and sent them on ahead of him, two by two, into every town and place where he himself was about to go. And he said to them, "The harvest is plentiful, but the laborers are few. Therefore pray earnestly to the Lord of the harvest to send out laborers into his harvest. Go your way; behold, I am sending you out as lambs in the midst of wolves. Carry no moneybag, no knapsack, no sandals, and greet no one on the road. Whatever house you enter, first say, 'Peace be to this house!' And if a son of peace is there, your peace will rest upon him. But if not, it will return to you.

And remain in the same house, eating and drinking what they provide, for the laborer deserves his wages. Do not go from house to house. Whenever you enter a town and they receive you, eat what is set before you. **Heal the sick in it and say to them, 'The kingdom of God has come near to you.'**

Jesus instructs to "tell them the Kingdom of God is near you" when they were manifesting these miracles. Tell them when this power is released that "The Kingdom of God is near you." Now, this seems cool for the exclusively New Testament reader, but if you have revelation from the Old Testament and the Prophets, this time in history meant so much more.

The Prophets prophesied about this day (when the Kingdom would come) and talked about when this happened, this dominion, power and government would grow until it eventually covered the entire earth. A mountain that rises high and covers the entire earth (see Daniel chapter 2), causing God's people to take possession of all the Kingdoms under the whole heavens (see Daniel 7:26-27), ushering in this current Eternal Kingdom Age! We are now actually living in an indestructible Eternal Kingdom Age!

Many people just read the New Testament like, "Cool Kingdom whatever." However, the people of that time who studied the Word, they're like "The Kingdom is here?!! You mean like God's people are about to take over?" That was their impression, and they showed that impression numerous times. Let's look at the book of Acts.

> Acts 1:6-8 They therefore, being come together, asked him saying, Lord, **is it at this time that thou restorest the kingdom to Israel?** And he said to them, It is not yours to know times or seasons, which the Father has placed in his own authority; but ye will receive power, the Holy Spirit having come upon you, and ye shall be my witnesses both in Jerusalem, and in all Judaea and Samaria, and to the end of the earth.

It's a process of growing until God's people take over the planet and we're back in charge. This is what God wants us to understand. This is what God needs the Church to grasp. We've been focusing on the wrong things. We've been focusing on the details like scripture and verse, rather than His story and His plan. These believers of the first century were believing for a Kingdom global takeover. Why? Because many of the Prophets taught this.

Let's go back now to Luke 10,

Luke 10:17 The seventy-two returned with joy, saying, **"Lord, even the demons are subject to us in your name!"**

It is interesting that this is the first thing the Disciples said when they returned from raising the dead, healing the sick and preaching the Kingdom. The thing they said was, "Hey, the demons are even subject to us in your name Jesus!!" Before Jesus emerged in His ministry they were pretty much hopeless against such demons, but all of a sudden, they're like, yeah whoa, these demons are subject to us in your name. And it's because a greater Kingdom had arrived!!! Then Jesus said something very key that you all must realize for the Kingdom message to make sense.

Jesus replied, "I saw satan fall like lightning from heaven" vs-18. He "saw" it; *past tense!* It already happened!! Now we don't know when exactly He saw it. But we do know that **Jesus said He saw satan fall from heaven before this point. This is important because that was over 2000 years ago.**

Why is this important? Well one reason is because people will read in the book of Revelation where it talks about the fall of satan, and they'll put it into the future. Right? Most people think that the book of Revelation is just a future book… They will say, well, Revelation talks about *when satan will fall.* Many ministers unfortunately are talking and teaching about *when satan falls,* like it is a future moment. NO!!! This is incorrect, because **satan has already fallen from heaven. He's fallen from his positioning, from his authority. He has no positioning except positioning that he has robbed from mankind.** The earth was given to man right? Not satan. And shortly I will be proving to you that all his authority has been stripped forever, and his judgment of guilty has already taken place.

Then let's go to Luke 10 one more time. If everyone could believe this one scripture, I am convinced that it would eliminate countless fears and cause the believer to walk in the life of victory.

> Luke 10:18-19 And he said to them, "**I saw satan fall like lightning from heaven.** Behold, I have given you authority to tread on serpents and scorpions, <u>and over all the power of the enemy, and nothing shall hurt you.</u>

Pause.

This one statement from Jesus crushes so many false prophecies. I just heard a prophecy yesterday where a guy said "Well, there's a prophecy fulfilled from back in the day that we were going to lose our freedoms, and it was going to continue to get worse and worse and worse, and we would never get them back." I said, "Lie. That is not true. Can't be true. The will of Heaven is coming to earth!!" **Heaven is invading earth, not hell!!**

See, that's the problem; too many doom and gloom teachings. I call them defeated gospels. These are the teachings where it is said God's people get defeated and things are supposed to get worse and worse. How are things to get worse and worse if the will of Heaven is invading this earth???? Isn't Heaven glorious? If the meek are inheriting the earth...?

The Gospel is Good News. Actually it is great news and I will prove it to you! It's probably much better than you have ever imagined!

Many Prophets of past generations, and even our current generation that were really on point with a lot of truths also believed this wrong theology of doom and gloom. They were and some still are living in the wrong AEON – meaning AGE. So they prophesied some weird stuff. Then people started believing it and thinking that things are going to get worse and worse. How are things supposed to get worse and worse when we have authority and power over all the powers of the enemy? When you don't follow Christ life is rough and things can get worse and worse. But when you do follow Christ, all of the devils are under your feet. The Bible says: nothing shall by any means harm you, we are always led in triumph in Christ, we are more than conquerors, that we are going from glory to glory!!! GLORY! We are supposed to be believing for and speaking for better and better, not worse and worse.

There are many believers that God gives a position of influence and they're speaking to large groups of people influencing and inspiring change for the better in the minds and hearts of humanity. They begin to stand up for truth, or expose evil and they think that they're going to get backlash and attacked. They even speak it out. "Oh they are gonna come after me for this one" some commonly say. They are expecting it, prophesying it on themselves. They get up to this high place of influence and favor and then by their words condemn themselves. Saying things like, "Yeah, but I know that the media is going to get me for this" or "They're gonna kill me for this one" and on and on.

This is fear and is in opposition to the truth. The truth is we have power and authority to overcome all the powers of the enemy nothing shall by any means hurt us. We must believe this truth and watch our mouths, to rise to the fullest potential God has for us and free this earth from it's bondage to corruption.

I know that I'm going to overcome the enemy always, he cannot overcome me. I have already been overcome by Christ Jesus! I have been purchased by His blood and have been made a King that reigns on this earth!! You can't be thinking the enemy's coming after you. The enemy needs to be thinking "Oh no, these believers are coming after me…" If you have all authority to overcome him, then get to overcoming!!!

This is what God has put in my heart that needs to shift radically in the earth. He wants to elevate us, but we cannot let our words give the enemy access to us. We can't be doing that. How are we as God's people, God's Kings, to rise up in this earth while saying things like, "Oh I know I'm gonna get killed for saying this." Yup you probably will get killed if you continue on talking like that. Don't you know a person's whole course of life is guided by their tongue? You are either freed or bound by your words. Brothers and sisters "keep a watch over your mouth." Speak words that serve and elevate you, not destroy you!

We're not going to get killed. We're not going to get overcome by the devil. We are crushing him and removing him off the face of this earth, while prospering and enjoying life with our families! That is the reality for those living in the victorious

revelation of the Gospel of the Kingdom. Now shout it out!! I LIVE IN VICTORY IN JESUS NAME!!!
I've had many times where I preach that the devil has been judged. It's one of my favorite messages. You know John 16 says when the Holy Spirit comes, He's going to reprove the world in regards to three things. SIN, RIGHTEOUSNESS, and JUDGMENT. The Holy Spirit loves to talk about the truth that satan has already been judged.

When some believers hear my message they say, "Cory, you can't talk like that or the devil will come after you." I say he doesn't come after me. I actually got him on the run, on defense, anxious, trying to keep my message in a box to no avail. If he does try something, he tries it from far away through somebody else. I will identify it and crush it if it is blocking my way.

> John 16:11 "of judgment, **because the ruler of this world is judged."**

That's the thing we must realize and come to terms with, satan has already been judged and we have power over him to remove him and all his nature / residue off the face of the earth. We just need to realize these truths for complete victory. Don't let satan intimidate you one day more. If you identify the

enemy trying to stop you from doing something, you manifest it out more, get it out there. I always say, "bully the bully, call his bluff and crush him."
Okay, let's continue now. So, Jesus sent out His disciples, gave them authority, they had power over the devil. This is all awesome news to a world of people who were sitting in darkness awaiting a savior!

Next point. I want and need to confirm to you that the word Kingdom means: Dominion, to Rule and Reign, or to Govern. Ready?

Let's go to Luke 19. And I'm going to read this one in the NLT version. If you're ever curious about the **Kingdom message,** or what the Kingdom means, Luke 19, is your reference point.

> Luke 19:11 The crowd was listening to everything Jesus said, and because he was nearing Jerusalem, **he told them a story to correct the impression that the kingdom of God would begin right away.**

Okay, you have to pause so you can absorb this. Jesus is telling this parable of the ten stewards because they were getting near to Jerusalem and **he needed to correct their impression that the kingdom of God would start right away.** They thought that once they got to Jerusalem they were going to take over the whole area with God's people, because that's what the prophets talked about. Almost every single prophet was prophesying of a day when a savior would come in judgment on Jerusalem, and then the people of God would take over. So, He's telling this story to correct their impression about how the Kingdom is to manifest.

They didn't correctly interpret the Prophets and they didn't fully understand Kingdom. Jesus is explaining what the Kingdom is in this chapter. The mystery is revealed, as well as how the Kingdom / Dominion manifests. This should be preached all the time. This Luke Chapter 19:11-26 should be preached all the time in the Churches so people can understand how Kingdom and God's Government on the earth operates and manifests.

As a matter of fact, this parable is preached all the time, but mostly misunderstood, skipping over the massive revelation of what Kingdom is and how Kingdom manifests!! We are not going to miss the point of this today.

Let's read it,

Luke 19:12-17 He said therefore, "A nobleman went into a far country to receive for himself a kingdom and then return. Calling ten of his servants, he gave them ten minas, and said to them, 'Engage in business until I come.' But his citizens hated him and sent a delegation after him, saying, 'We do not want this man to reign over us.' When he returned, having received the kingdom, he ordered these servants to whom he had given the money to be called to him, that he might know what they had gained by doing business. The first came before him, saying, 'Lord, your mina has made ten minas more.' And he said to him, 'Well done, good servant! **Because you have been faithful in a very little, <u>you shall have authority (charge) over ten cities.'</u>**

You shall have authority / charge / dominion / government over ten cities. Make sure to study out that word "take authority over cities" in different versions especially the Greek or Hebrew Concordance to get it locked in your mind and heart!!! Important parts like this need personal word study. (Interlinear-Bible with a Strong's Concordance is what I recommend.)

Let's keep going, so where do we hear that in preaching today? Take charge of cities??! That's what we're supposed to be talking about. If you haven't read the Old Testament, and you don't know the promise of Abraham then this doesn't make sense to you. You might be like, "what cities? Why would we need cities?" Trust me we need cities, but I will expound more soon. However, this was the promise God gave to Abraham, "Your descendants will take possession of the cities of their enemies and all nations will be blessed." We will get there shortly, and this will all be connecting, so take notes, remove as many distractions as you can, and focus. Some very good news is coming.

So, Jesus is saying in this parable that the way the Kingdom manifests is through stewards who can cause multiplication for the master; they will be given authority of cities, a.k.a. government over territories. Are you starting to get it!?? The Kingdom message is a takeover message, but not an instantaneous manifestation like they had thought.

It's even more than just possessing cities. It's about possessing *the gates of our enemies* (places of highest power in the earth). It's about possessing nations as the people of God. We will surely get to talk more on this in a future chapter, but for now I am just going to pause here so you can reflect on Luke 19. I want you to realize Jesus was explaining what the Kingdom is like and how it comes to this group of people. It comes through those who are faithful and wise stewards and through those who can multiply things for the Lord. They are to take charge of or govern of cities.

I think people also miss the part about, **the multiplying of things.** You know, once you grow in the Kingdom your mind will start to think in multiplication. I remember when I first started prospering financially, I realized the idea of digital courses and how I could put one out and it could work for me by multiplying my efforts. Instead of me teaching the same thing over and over and over as addition, I realized I should think multiplication. Then my mind moved to more multiplication. Now I'm multiplying all kinds of things including many types of plants, trees, sheep, goats, and even dogs, GLORY!

So, these stewards, the Lord checks in on them and then He says, "Well done, take charge over ten cities." Taking charge is taking Dominion. Taking Dominion is taking Kingdom. Luke 19 is talking about how the Dominion of God, given to his servants, is to manifest and free this earth from evil through the righteous rising to power.

See most people miss this because they don't think that the Kingdom message has anything to do with taking possession of land, nor do they think about being leaders of this earth as God's Children. Most believers have been wrapped up in false ideas like rapture and destruction, rather than rebuilding, renewing, restoring, and governing this earth.

If you decide to be a wise, faithful steward, the Lord shows up and sees what you've done. Then He knows if He can trust you. It's a genius way to draw out who is qualified to rule the world, right? Give them all a little and the ones who did good, caused multiplication for the Lord, let them take charge of cities and become the Kings of the earth. Those who do bad, take what they have and give it to the one who does good!!

But what I'm really hoping you guys get is this, that the Lord must approve, and THEN SPEAK OVER THE BELIEVER "TAKE CHARGE." It is a Word that not all believers have had spoken on their life. They must first be tested. But once that Word of approval comes, watch out. I am also convinced that there are many who have this approval but are at the same time believing it is the end of the world. Believing it is the end of the world is not going to give you much motivation to take charge of cities.

The Kingdom is the power God gave us to govern this earth. This is what we're supposed to understand as the body of Christ, that we have Dominion now!! Even before, the disciples had Dominion in the name of Jesus! But there's another level, a level where you enter in and God speaks over your life, and you become a Ruler, a King, a Governor over cities and nations. And this is where we need to get to in our level of revelation and manifestation. I believe this will happen swiftly as this Kingdom seed of truth spreads in hearts around the world.

> Galatians 3:8 And the Scripture, **foreseeing that God would justify the Gentiles by faith, preached** <u>the gospel</u> **beforehand to Abraham, saying,** <u>"In you shall all the nations be blessed."</u>

I am convinced that God has spoken this "take charge" "take Kingdom" already over some believers in this earth. And He's spoken it over some people that don't know what they're supposed to do with it. **I have encountered someone that I know has this Word of "Well done, take charge" spoken over him.** My wife and I both saw it.

We were up in this mountain community of Nicaragua and I came to know a guy in charge of many things. This guy owns giant farms on hundreds of acres, jungle farms of coffee, bananas, oranges, and plantains. He has hundreds of workers and is quite prosperous. He and his wife are Holy Ghost filled. Actually the whole family is filled with the Holy Ghost!! They are just awesome, and he is amazing. I'm still friends with him and respect him very much. One day I was like, "Brother, you're supposed to be the mayor of this city. It's written all over your face." My wife says the same thing. "You're supposed to be the mayor of the city." And he says, "Those positions are for the devil and his people. Politics is for the devil, not the people of God." I was kinda shocked to hear him say this because he is a very smart man.

I said, "So is it better to have a devil in charge of a city, or a son or daughter of God?" He had no answer. He had been raised up with the theology that things are supposed to get worse and worse (end times), not brighter and brighter as the will of Heaven comes to earth. We must not continue in this error any longer.

Okay. What I'm saying is that there are believers with this special Word of trust that the Lord gives saying "Well done my faithful steward, take charge of cities" but they don't understand the Kingdom Message and never step out to fulfill God's perfect will of reconciling the world (Kosmos – all of the earth and its inhabitants) back to himself in Christ. They understand religion. They understand false theology, thinking that it's the end of the world. When the Bible's talking about the end of an age, the age of Moses, where God lived in a temple. Now He lives in us and we are in the eternal age of the Kings of God!

The Kings of God are now here on the earth, rising up through revelation and manifesting to set creation free from its bondage to corruption! All of creation is waiting for us to come together and get this!

Wow, you know, God told me this one time, "I never thought that my people would get so far off base." I'm convinced that God told me that it never crossed His mind, that His people would start thinking He was going to destroy the whole planet." Oh my, how off course has the Church been, until now. We are taking back our inheritance!! This earth!

We must keep it simple. We must keep focused with what we do know and not living by assumptions. We do know that Jesus taught us to pray "Thy kingdom come, Thy will be done on earth, as it is in Heaven." The devil, we just saw, fell from Heaven. He is not in Heaven anymore. And Jesus said, "Let your will be done on the earth as it is in Heaven." That means that the devil is also supposed to be off the face of the earth as well. There are no wicked leaders in Heaven, let this be so on the earth as well. Amen.

Okay, we're almost done here. Matthew 5:5 let's go there real quick for reference.

> Matthew 5:5 "Blessed are the meek, **for they shall <u>inherit</u> the earth.**"

That word **inherit** is very important. There are so many religious movements out there today that talk about our inheritance.. Only they RARELY talk about the **earth as our inheritance.** I'm telling you they'll talk about everything else, making up stuff that sounds all spiritual, when the reality is that we are <u>heirs</u> or <u>inheritors of this planet.</u> The inheritance is the earth. We are co-heirs with Christ. That means we are co-heirs of the earth. We have to keep it simple. The meek will inherit the earth. This earth is ours! And most of the Church has been taught a lie. As a matter of fact, most theologies today don't line up with the meek inheriting this earth. They say this earth is to be destroyed. Why? Misunderstanding of God's story. Preaching scripture and verse without looking at the whole picture.

Let's go to Matthew 13 really quick,

> Matthew 13:31-32 He put another parable before them, saying, "The kingdom of heaven is like a grain of mustard seed that a man took and sowed in his field. **It is the smallest of all seeds, but when it has grown it is larger than all the garden**

plants and becomes a tree, so that the birds of the air come and make nests in its branches.

This revelation, or this Message of the Kingdom may seem like a small matter at first. It may seem insignificant as you first start talking about the Kingdom message. **But Holy Ghost has a way of making this seed stick in hearts,** and when this seed sticks it begins to grow until it's the biggest most important revelation in your life. I have seen it happen many times. You will begin to wonder, why and how are so many people missing this? This revelation of Kingdom expansion and Kingdom takeover is all throughout the Word. You will begin to see it everywhere. Just make sure you water this seed and share what you learn. Stay teachable and humble towards the Holy Spirit, our teacher, and you will bare much fruit.

Make sure to not get your feelings hurt when people tell you you're wrong or call you names, good people do this sometimes. Why? Well, this message is great news, but they have accepted doom and gloom and tried to make it good news in their imaginations. Some will listen, some will not. Just remember, they haven't read these 150 or so scriptures laid out here in this story/study of God's will. They might have only heard chapters and verses scattered throughout their lives. But regardless, we need to have tougher skin, not worry about what others think, do what we know to be right, and get this truth out. All of creation is waiting for the revealing of the children of God. No more "political correctness." That's a sneaky trick of the enemy to keep good people from speaking the truth boldly.

Once a person gets this revelation, everything changes. You become rooted in as an oak of righteousness, a planting of the Lord for the display of his splendor, unstoppable.

> Isaiah 61:3 In their righteousness, they will be like great oaks that the Lord has planted for his own glory (splendor).

The birds of the air, spoken of in the parable of the sower, that come and perch in the branches are the wandering ones trying to find truth and stability. They have been from place to place in search of truth. Wandering and hearing messages from those who are only along the path. But now once this Kingdom stabilization (as an oak of righteousness) takes place, these birds (new believers) find Kingdom truth and a place to perch, rest, and learn while dwelling in spiritual protection. Yes, we are able to spiritually branch out and provide security for believers, that is a part of Kingship. "Why?" you may ask? It's because we know the message, we understand the Kingdom plan, we understand that we cannot be touched by evil or overcome by evil. So, if tyrants rise up around us they're going to fall. Eventually there will be no more tyrants at all on this planet which I can prove as well. It doesn't matter what comes against us, we are always going to win. Our minds have been trained to do so. We take on the "all I do is win" mentality because we know we are in the will, we know we are called, and we know that all things are working together for our good!

We are oaks of righteousness, a planting of the Lord for the display of his splendor / glory!

In essence that is what the Kingdom Message is, we win! We who are doing the will of the Father will always win, we will always be led in victory! God is raising up His kings right now. They actually believe the Word and believe to the fullest. We're taking over and nothing can stop us. GLORY!

Next, I use this scripture a lot when preaching the Kingdom message,

Matthew 13:33 Jesus also used this illustration: "The Kingdom of Heaven is like the yeast a woman used in making bread. Even though she put only a little yeast in three measures of flour, **it permeated every part of the dough."**

"It permeated every part." **The Kingdom "permeated every part."** So don't tell me things are getting worse and worse. You see now? How are things supposed to get worse and worse when the Kingdom of God is permeating every part? You know what's happening? The devil is getting exposed, and many are getting shaken up right now because they have been way off, and speaking way off over their lives.

But now the Kingdom message has a perfect chance to finally enter in the hearts of the believers. A perfect chance to slide in because people who were in church hearing this doom and gloom stuff are now seeing their doom and gloom in front of their face. The pandemic and all this other stuff being exposed in the years 2019-2022. They need some power, they need some Kingdom, **they need some purpose.** And now is the time to realize the Kingdom message! **They need the Truth that sets Nations Free!!**

This scripture explains the Kingdom message well. It's like yeast, it is a Kingdom takeover! You will get it soon, just stick with me! Let me ask you something. Do you think that Jesus used this yeast parable because He was studying the prophecies and saw other similar prophecies?!

Maybe a prophecy like this one?

> Daniel 2:44 And in the days of these kings shall the God of the heavens set up a kingdom which shall never be destroyed; and the sovereignty thereof shall not be left to another people: **it shall break in pieces and <u>consume all these kingdoms,</u> but <u>itself shall stand for ever.</u>**

Or maybe He was influenced by this prophecy?

> Isaiah 9:6-7 For unto us a child is born, unto us a son is given; and the government shall be upon His shoulder; and His name is called Wonderful, Counselor, Mighty God, Father of Eternity, Prince of Peace. **Of the increase of His government and of <u>peace there shall be no end,</u>** upon the throne of David and over His kingdom, to establish it, and to uphold it with judgment and with righteousness, **<u>from henceforth even forever.</u>** The zeal of Jehovah of hosts will perform this.

I now need to explain something. I need to bring to light what I've been saying in regard to "mankind always had the Kingdom / Dominion from God" we just couldn't use it.

> Luke 17:20-21 One day the Pharisees asked Jesus, "When will the Kingdom of God come?" Jesus replied, "The Kingdom of God can't be detected by visible signs. You won't be able to say, 'Here it is!' or 'It's over there!' **For the Kingdom of God is already among (within) you."**

Wait, did Jesus just say the Kingdom of God is already among, some versions say within, the Pharisees? Regardless, Jesus is telling the Pharisees that the Kingdom is with them before the cross!?? But that doesn't fit any theologies I have heard in the churches. Well, it makes perfect sense if you understand that Kingdom is the dominion God spoke over mankind in the beginning.

He spoke it over them, and they went the wrong direction following the wrong spirit. And like I said before, Dominion or Kingdom doesn't function with sin. It doesn't function until a person is "born again from above" as the righteousness of God. Even the Pharisees had Kingdom within / among them, but they couldn't use it. **Dominion was spoken over mankind, but they needed a savior, they needed to be born again.**

BUT NOW... Jesus came and reconciled us. Okay. Reconcile. That's a big word that we're going to talk about soon. He reconciled us back to the Father, back to The Blessing, back to The Dominion, back to The Garden, back to the positioning before sin. So, what does that mean for us? What does it look like? Well, we need to start identifying ourselves as reconciled back unto God before sin, where we have dominion, where we are fruitful, and where we are free from the toilet system – I mean toil system.

We are out of that toil system now in Christ, but we must renew our minds to this reality and be transformed by it! We are reconciled back to The Garden, back to The Blessing, back to The Glory, back to Righteousness, and now we are learning to use our ability to operate as the Kings of God. We are purchased by the Blood of Jesus to be Kings and Priests that Reign on earth! So, let's get to reigning.

Revelation 5:9-10 And they sing a new song, saying, Thou art worthy to take the book, and to open its seals; because Thou hast been slain, a**nd hast redeemed to God, by Thy blood, out of every tribe, and tongue, and people, and nation, <u>and made them to our God kings and priests; and they shall reign over the earth.</u>**

Toil is a lie for all of those who believe in Jesus and do the will of the Father. Toil is the life of never enough, the life Adam experienced outside of the Garden. I'm here to teach you that we in Christ, have been reconciled back to the Garden!! This is really good news, once you get this revelation and choose to believe it, everything changes!

Recap, we are wrapping up here in just a second. So, I already mentioned this, we have the Kingdom of God, **which is the power of God to rule and reign as Kings with righteousness, peace, and joy in the Holy Ghost. It's the power, authority, and blessing of God manifesting.** The Kingdom of God is the dominion of God!!

Now that you know WHAT THE KINGDOM IS, next you need to know more about the Story of God which is so beautiful. This story is called **"The Message of the Kingdom."**

This is what we are going to be diving into, and what I hope to get the world to realize. We need to understand the Message of the Kingdom. This revelation and story will be coming forth in our next few chapters. However, I'm going to give you a couple more things to better prepare you for our next chapter.

Matthew 13:18-19 "Now listen to the explanation of the parable about the farmer planting seeds: The seed that fell on the footpath represents those who hear **the message about the Kingdom and don't understand it.** Then the evil one comes and snatches away the seed that was planted in their hearts.

You will have people say, "well, the Kingdom of God is not in talk." Right? Scripture says this in regard to the raw power manifesting, okay? Yeah. When you're manifesting power, it is not just talking, it is actually manifesting power. **But there's a message of the Kingdom, which is the story of God and the purpose of God. It is why you and I are here!**

Make sure you focus, take notes, <u>and understand</u> the things we're about to learn. Once you understand the Kingdom seed takes root, that's when you get that bountiful harvest of Kingdom Fruit (Dominion Fruit)! The message of the Kingdom is what freaks the devil out. He tries to steal the message, so it doesn't take root in people's hearts and grow and crush his systems.

I am asking you to value what you are about to learn, water what you learn, re-read what you learn, take notes, and TAKE ROOT!! The Kingdom Message manifests the most fruit! You see, satan isn't so worried about the message about gifts of the Spirit.

Actually, he is somewhat. He doesn't like tongues, *but he's looking for the Message of the Kingdom. He doesn't want people to get this message because it means the end of him,* and it's clear today that he is really going after this message. So, you guys want to know the "message of the Kingdom" in just two scriptures?!

There are two scriptures that plainly tell the Kingdom message. You don't have to demystify it. You just have to hear it and believe it! This is it. It is found in Daniel 7. **Remember these 2 verses your whole life, cherish them, they are ours!** In the next chapter we will open up this revelation even more!

> Daniel 7:26-27 "But then the court will pass judgment, and all his power will be taken away and completely destroyed. **Then the sovereignty, power, and greatness of all the kingdoms under heaven will be given to the holy people (the Saints) of the Most High. His kingdom will last forever, and all rulers will serve and obey him.**"

Meditate on the above scripture and you will be putting the seed of the message of the Kingdom into your heart. If you ever forget what the Kingdom Message is, just come right back here to Daniel 7:26-27.

Paint that picture in your imagination, all kingdoms under the whole heavens being handed over to the saints of God, all rulers worshiping and obeying God!!! Kick out all this other weird stuff about flying off the earth, and doom and gloom. Get the picture in your imagination of all rulers on the planet serving, worshiping, and obeying God. All nations being blessed. All of Heaven invading and infusing with the earth and its inhabitants! Oh, my!! Good news!!

See this now. Jesus entered Heaven after He arose from the grave and they opened a book and sung a new song that says, we are Kings and Priests that have been purchased by the Blood, that shall reign on the earth. The court has sat, which means we're supposed to be believing it's our time to take over this world "all the kingdoms under the whole heavens will be handed over to the saints."

People say, "Cory if this is true, why don't we see it?" Well simple, because many people aren't preaching and teaching it, therefore many are not believing for it. Faith comes by hearing. When we understand and believe the truth of God's story and His Promise, we will begin manifesting these prophecies at light speed! It's coming!

CH.2 RECONCILED BACK TO THE GARDEN

Alright, we're going to start right in the beginning of Genesis for this chapter. It says,

> Genesis 2:4-17 These are the generations of the heavens and the earth when they were created, in the day that the Lord God made the earth and the heavens.

When no bush of the field was yet in the land and no small plant of the field had yet sprung up—for the Lord God had not caused it to rain on the land, and there was no man to work the ground, and a mist was going up from the land and was watering the whole face of the ground— then the Lord God formed the man of dust from the ground and breathed into his nostrils the breath of life, and the man became a living creature. And the Lord God planted a garden in Eden, in the east, and there he put the man whom he had formed. And out of the ground the Lord God made to spring up every tree that is pleasant to the sight and good for food. The tree of life was in the midst of the garden, and the tree of the knowledge of good and evil.

A river flowed out of Eden to water the garden, and there it divided and became four rivers. The name of the first is the Pishon. It is the one that flowed around the whole land of Havilah, where there is gold. And the gold of that land is good; bdellium and onyx stone are there. The name of the second river is the Gihon. It is the one that flowed around the whole land of Cush. And the name of the third river is the Tigris, which flows east of Assyria. And the fourth river is the Euphrates.

The Lord God took the man and put him in the garden of Eden to work it and keep it. And the Lord God commanded the man, saying, "You may surely eat of every tree of the garden, but of the tree of the knowledge of good and evil you shall not eat, for in the day that you eat of it you shall surely die."

God decided to put the man in His Garden that He created. He could have put him in lots of places, but he put him in a Garden, why? Well let's find out. See, our original purpose is to be stewards of the earth, managers, and workers of the earth / soil. That's why God created us. He created all the earth and then He decided to put a man in His image and likeness to work the earth. So, He planted a Garden and put man in it with the hope that he would

expand, multiply, be fruitful, subdue the land, replenish it, stock it with abundance, take this good seed, take this good Garden and fill the earth. He and his family would multiply in the earth. That was the plan, right? But don't eat of that tree. And as you know, he ate of the tree, him, and his wife. So, God kicked them out of the Garden and then cut off the access to the Garden with a flaming sword held by a Cherubim.

Next, I want to say something. **Most people do not still think we were put on the earth to "work it and take care of it."** When I was running the water system for my farm recently, I ran four long branches. We have at least 500 meters worth of water lines to water the whole farm. Why did I do this? Well because I want to make the whole area a giant garden. I've been telling God; this is my Garden of Eden. We are actually building our own Garden of Eden, and in a little while I will tell you why this is in my heart to do. Oh yeah, and after only one and a half years we have around 25 goats and sheep, and all of my females of age are pregnant. We also have a house that is completely off grid, and have planted around 1,200 fruit trees. It is coming along with the grace of God!!! I share this with you not to brag, but because I want you to know I am living and believing what I am about to teach you. I am not just talking some fairy tale. We in Christ are to be reconciled back to Dominion, reconciled back to the Blessing, reconciled back to the Garden! Rebuild, renew, restore, replenish the earth!

Reconciliation is a beautiful force of Divine Favor from Heaven. We are reconciled says the Word of God. But reconciled to what exactly??

Let's keep going and find out,

> Genesis 2:17 "but of the tree of the knowledge of good and evil you shall not eat, for in the day that you eat of it you shall surely die."

Adam and Eve were not created to die, but to live forever.

Genesis 2:18-25 Then the Lord God said, "It is not good that the man should be alone; I will make him a helper fit for him." Now out of the ground the Lord God had formed every beast of the field and every bird of the heavens and brought them to the man to see what he would call them. And whatever the man called every living creature, that was its name. The man gave names to all livestock and to the birds of the heavens and to every beast of the field. But for Adam there was not found a helper fit for him. So, the Lord God caused a deep sleep to fall upon the man, and while he slept took one of his ribs and closed up its place with flesh. And the rib that the Lord God had taken from the man he made into a woman and brought her to the man. Then the man said,

"This at last is bone of my bones
and flesh of my flesh;
she shall be called Woman,
because she was taken out of Man."

Therefore, a man shall leave his father and his mother and hold fast to his wife, and they shall become one flesh. And the man and his wife were both naked and were not ashamed.

Alright next to we need to read this chapter together to understand how this all ties into the Kingdom Message and our Reconciliation back to the Garden!

Genesis 3 The serpent was the shrewdest of all the wild animals the Lord God had made. One day he asked the woman, "Did God really say you must not eat the fruit from any of the trees in the garden?"

"Of course we may eat fruit from the trees in the garden," the woman replied. "It's only the fruit from the tree in the middle of the garden that we are not allowed to eat. God said, 'You must not eat it or even touch it; if you do, you will die.'"

"You won't die!" the serpent replied to the woman. "God knows that your eyes will be opened as soon as you eat it, and you will be like God, knowing both good and evil."

The woman was convinced. She saw that the tree was beautiful, and its fruit looked delicious, and she wanted the wisdom it would give her. So, she took some of the fruit and ate it. Then she gave some to her husband, who was with her, and he ate it, too. At that moment their eyes were opened, and they suddenly felt shame at their nakedness. So, they sewed fig leaves together to cover themselves.

When the cool evening breezes were blowing, the man and his wife heard the Lord God walking about in the garden. So they hid from the Lord God among the trees. Then the Lord God called to the man, "Where are you?"

He replied, "I heard you walking in the garden, so I hid. I was afraid because I was naked." "Who told you that you were naked?" the Lord God asked. "Have you eaten from the tree whose fruit I commanded you not to eat?" The man replied, "It was the woman you gave me who gave me the fruit, and I ate it." Then the Lord God asked the woman, "What have you done?" "The serpent deceived me," she replied. "That's why I ate it."

Then the Lord God said to the serpent,
"Because you have done this, you are cursed more than all animals, domestic and wild. You will crawl on your belly, groveling in the dust as long as you live. And I will cause hostility between you and the woman, and between your offspring and her offspring. He will strike your head, and you will strike his heel."

Then he said to the woman,
"I will sharpen the pain of your pregnancy, and in pain you will give birth. And you will desire to control your husband, but he will rule over you."

And to the man he said,

"Since you listened to your wife and ate from the tree whose fruit I commanded you not to eat, the ground is cursed because of you. All your life you will struggle to scratch a living from it. It will grow thorns and thistles for you, though you will eat of its grains. By the sweat of your brow will you have food to eat until you return to the ground from which you were made. For you were made from dust and to dust you will return."

Then the man—Adam—named his wife Eve because she would be the mother of all who live. And the Lord God made clothing from animal skins for Adam and his wife.

Then the Lord God said, "Look, the human beings have become like us, knowing both good and evil. What if they reach out, take fruit from the tree of life, and eat it? Then they will live forever!" **So the Lord God banished them from the Garden of Eden, and he sent Adam out to cultivate the ground from which he had been made. After sending them out, the Lord God stationed mighty cherubim to the east of the Garden of Eden. And he placed a flaming sword that flashed back and forth to guard the way to the tree of life.**

Now that we have this chapter in our hearts we can move forward. Next, we are going to go to the famous verse John 3:16, I bet many of you can quote it, but how many of you can quote the next verse, verse 17? I wish so much that people would do a word study on verse 17. Let's go there.

> John 3:16-17 "For God so loved the world, that He gave His only Son, that whoever believes in Him should not perish but have eternal life. **For God did not send His Son into the world to condemn the world, but in order that the world might be saved through Him.**"

Now, that verse 17, I see why most people stop at 16 because verse 17 doesn't fit what is taught in the Church. They say God needs to destroy this earth, and that things are to get worse and worse. No, no, no. God says He so loved this world that He sent His Son to save the world. Now what we need to realize is that word "world" does not mean only people. We've taken the gospel, and we've made it only about saving people. But this is about saving the world, the planet, the Kosmos, it's always been about the Kosmos.

If you do a Greek search on the word "World" here, you will find the word "Kosmos" and the definition of that word is "all of God's created ordered system including its inhabitants." See God sent his son to reconcile the PLANET and THE PEOPLE back to Himself. If you look up the word "save" the world, you will find the word "sozo." The definition of that word is saved, healed, delivered, made whole, restored.

So, God wants to save, heal, and reconcile the whole world NOT JUST PEOPLE. He wants to save the whole world, not just people!! That is the piece that has been missing from the teaching in the Churches. This is the missing piece of the puzzle that has allowed Christians to sit idly by while evil seeks to destroy the planet.

Now that we got that figured out, we're going to let the scriptures tell the story and then we'll talk. Let's go to the book of 2nd Corinthians.

> 2 Corinthians 5:16-19 From now on, therefore, we regard no one according to the flesh. Even though we once regarded Christ according to the flesh, we regard him thus no longer. Therefore, if anyone is in Christ, he is a new creation. The old has passed away; behold, the new has come. All this is from God, who through **Christ reconciled us to Himself and gave us the ministry of reconciliation; that is, in Christ God was**

reconciling the world (KOSMOS) to Himself, not counting their trespasses against them, and entrusting to us the message of reconciliation.

If anyone is in Christ, they are a new creation, meaning born again, something new, born from above not of natural descent. And we'll learn later that you're born again as a King by the blood of Jesus Christ. This part is super exciting!

We're going to get into an amazing truth right now. The Word says that He "reconciled us to Himself." What does this mean? The word reconciled, is the word "katallagē" in the Greek with various uses in 2 Corinthians 5 which is worth studying out. However, this word signifies "to be brought back to an original positioning" "an original positioning of divine favor and connection to Heaven."

This is the place where Adam was, in the Garden of Eden, before he sinned. He was in a position of divine favor, flowing in harmony with God, in harmony with Heaven, in harmony with creation, no evil, everything good, everything producing and with abundance. He had no issues. He was in the divine favor, in harmony with Heaven in the Garden!!! How glorious it must have been. How glorious it can be for us now my friends!

We are reconciled to this same positioning and even better now because of Jesus, as well as the mighty men of faith such as David and Abraham who also through their faithfulness imparted powerful precious promises to us. However, we must renew our mind to transform our reality into this **Truth of Reconciled.** We are reconciled and empowered as ministers of reconciliation, bringing all of the creation back to the Father.

But it says we are reconciled back to God. Okay, well, let's keep reading here. It says "God who reconciled us to Himself through Christ and gave us the ministry of reconciliation, that God was reconciling the world to himself in Christ. There's that word "world" again. See this is where the Church has been lacking in its revelation, please understand. When most believers read this and see the word "world" they think it is talking about God just reconciling worldly people, however it's not. Do a Greek word study yourself.

The word used is "Kosmos" not people, Kosmos is a much bigger word that encompasses all of God's creation. "Let's go out and save people today!!" Great idea, but do we keep throwing trash on the streets? Do we keep chopping down all the trees and not replacing them, do we keep eating food without planting any, do we keep hunting animals without multiplying them?? See we must think of these things to be good stewards and workers of the earth. God put mankind here in the first place to work His Garden, right?? Do you have a garden?? If not now is the time to begin, there is no greater connection to the Father than in the Garden. He loves to Garden, and to speak to those who share this joy with Him.

> John 15:1 "I am the true grapevine, and **my Father is the gardener."**

I saw an article the other day and it was titled something like "Where have all the bees gone?" I was thinking to myself, "Well they have come to my house." My house is full of beautiful bees; well my garden I should say. We have sunflowers growing just for them. A sunflower can feed a group of bees for months while they pollinate all our other fruits and vegetables.

Then I thought to myself again, "The real question isn't 'where are all the bees,' the question is where are all the gardeners? the flower planters??" This is the issue, not some strange conspiracy of disappearing bees. Think about it for a second. How many people do you know that plant flowers for the bees? The great pollinators of our earth? Most people would rather kill them, or just extract their honey. In my family we live in harmony with them, and they don't try to sting us. Why you wonder? Well, reconciliation is also the process of bringing you back into harmony with ALL of God's creation. See the bees didn't have a great fall and the birds didn't sin against God and get thrown out of harmony. It was only humanity that fell from this blessed connection to God and His creation. God is reconciling us back into harmony with all His creation.

In today's day some people would say I'm crazy for having bees around my house. Well, I think it is crazy to be so disconnected from nature to not know the answer to "where have all the bees gone?" Bees like flowers. If you stop planting flowers you won't see bees!!! Plant some lovely sunflowers for them and you will see them come. The other day in the backyard at my house (near the city) we have a new patch of about 20 sunflowers and none of them are with flowers yet, however I saw the bees coming in to check on them and waiting for the buds to open. Our house is literally in the middle of what some would call a desert, and somehow the bees know that in this one yard there is a flower about to bloom. Amazing!

Our backyard is filled with all kinds of beautiful lettuces and tomatoes, onions, herbs, and fruit trees sprouting up to go to the farm, and of course sunflowers. I get a huge family salad each day out of this yard if I like. Things that are impossible to get at the local or commercial supermarket. All you need is some seed, sun, and water!! Get connected to nature, that is why you were created. Make sure you get some organic seed too by the way.

Sad to say, but most of the Church is completely disconnected from nature because of their *end times* views. God is not destroying this earth He is reconciling it back to Himself in Christ. God so loved this world that He sent His one and only Son to "sozo" it not destroy it. I hope that you can see this and erase the damaging idea that the planet is going to be destroyed out of your heart. In the coming chapters I will explain more and you will see it is not the end times. The end times was the end of the Age of Moses and the Temple Worship system. People under the law had to worship in the Temple in Jerusalem and that time has ended. That was the end of an age. The King James Bible version got it wrong when it said end of the world (Matthew 24:3), it was the end of an age (AEON) not end of the world (Kosmos). BIG DIFFERENCE RIGHT!!?

Many are now realizing that the end times was the end of the Temple Worship system set up in Jerusalem. That age ended in 70 a.d. when the Temple was destroyed by Roman armies which ushered in the new and eternal Kingdom Age.

However many still believe we are in the last days of the planet.

One group is rebuilding, renewing, and restoring. The other group is mostly waiting on things to get worse and worse, and speaking it out.

Back to the Garden..

Unfortunately many people in the family of God are only consumers, we are called to be producers of fruit, multipliers of livestock, stocking the earth with abundance, blessing the nations and the generations to come.. Most make the incorrect conclusion that we are called to just produce spiritual fruit. But remember, God put Adam in a real garden and expected him to grow real fruit. How far we have gone off the course! Well we are to get back on track!!!

We need to realize that we cannot just keep taking, taking, and taking from the earth and not giving back. This is madness. However, Christians justify it with songs with lyrics like "forget this world just give me Jesus." They have this view because of an incorrect understanding of the heart and plan of God. How can we say "forget this world" when "God so loved this world He sent His one and only Son?" He says He gave us the ministry of reconciling the world, and that we are heirs of this world!!? So, if we're in Christ, don't you want to know what your ministry is? Reconciling the world back to the Father!! Not waiting for its destruction. Some people will still want to believe it is the end of the planet even though this book will more than prove that to be a lie. God so loved this world (kosmos) He sent His Son to save it, not condemn or destroy it.

God had to do away with sin on the cross. By now you should understand why Jesus became sin and nailed it to the cross, but let's talk about this for a moment. Sin caused God to say "Cursed now is the ground because of you." However, reconciliation and righteousness now say "Blessed now is the ground because of you." When you believe in Jesus and are baptized, you are no longer a sinner, you arise a new creation you become the righteousness of God. I'm putting this in here because I know many of you guys know this, but some may not.

When you believe in Christ Jesus and get baptized, your sin, and your old nature are all nailed to the cross. You get born again, as a King, a new creation. You are not a sinner, you don't have sin in you, you are a reconciled Son or Daughter of God. If you don't have sin in you, what does that mean? Where does that place you? It places you back in the Garden, RECONCILED back to your original positioning of divine favor and harmony with Heaven! I believe you are starting to get it! Renew your mind, transform your life! I am excited for all who have made it this far! You are the truth seekers and I believe great blessing is in store for you!

> Romans 5:9-11 Since, therefore, we have now been justified by His blood, much more shall we be saved by Him from the wrath of God. For if while we were enemies we were reconciled to God by the death of his Son, much more, now that we are reconciled, shall we be saved by His life. More than that, **we also rejoice in God through our Lord Jesus Christ, through whom we have now received reconciliation.**

Without sin in you guess what? There is no longer a toil system either. No longer do you have to work at the sweat of your brow, and it never be enough. All those things that were happening to Adam and Eve were because of sin; sin entered into them and the earth was responding back. Toil is the effect of sin, abundance is the effect of being born again from above as the righteousness of God and knowing His promises.

But now, Jesus became sin and nailed it to the cross removing it from us and making us new creations without sin. Your flesh and body may do things wrong, but your spirit cannot contain sin anymore. You have passed from death to life in Christ. So, what that means guys, I'm here to tell you that we are back in the Garden, now, and he has given us the Ministry of Reconciliation.

God is reconciling the world, the Kosmos, the whole planet back to Himself. And He committed to us the Message of Reconciliation. We are Christ Ambassadors, as though God we're making His appeal through us. We implore you on Christ's behalf be reconciled to God. God made Him who had no sin to be sin for us, so that in Him we might become the righteousness of God.

It is an amazing feeling to know our job description on this planet. Ministers of Reconciliation! If I were to ask 100 Christians what our ministry in Christ is, I wonder how many would say "We have the Ministry of Reconciliation, that God is reconciling the world back to Himself in Christ, not counting men's sins against them?" And then I wonder how many of them would know that the word "world" means (kosmos -

all of God's created ordered system – planet and inhabitants)?

Because of Adam's disobedience sin entered the ground on this planet, and earth was cursed. Everywhere sinners walk, the earth responds negatively to them. It is a frequency; sin is a frequency. It's a sporadic frequency that the earth doesn't like and the only solution to it is Jesus. Giving your life to Him. Laying down your will and picking up your Word to learn and do the will of the Father.

> Matthew 7:21-23 **"<u>Not everyone</u> who says to Me, 'Lord, Lord,' will enter the kingdom of heaven, <u>but the one who does the will of My Father who is in heaven.</u>** On that day many will say to me, 'Lord, Lord, did we not prophesy in your name, and cast out demons in your name, and do many mighty works in your name?' And then will I declare to them, 'I never knew you; depart from me, you workers of lawlessness.'

So now you should know the will of the Father, bring everything back into harmony with Him, and His divine favor, reconcile, rebuild, renew, restore, stock with abundance, steward the earth well, and multiply!! The objective of God is to destroy satan and all his nature off this earth, and have His Spirit be in all and through all, Heaven infused with earth and all its inhabitants! Simple. Now we must discover how we can co-labor with Him in making this world a better place. From the scripture above it shows that many think they are going the right way, but they are not. Only those who know the will of the Father and do it, will enter this divine Heavenly dominion and realm of the Father.

And so, the Bible says,

Romans 8:19-22 **For the creation waits with eager longing for the revealing of the sons of God.** For the creation was subjected to futility, not willingly, but because of him who subjected it, **in hope that the creation itself will be set free from its bondage to corruption and obtain the freedom of the glory of the children of God.** For we know that the whole creation has been groaning together in the pains of childbirth **until now.**

From this we can see that the children of God already have this "freedom of the Children of God." Therefore, the creation must be brought into the same glorious freedom we have. Yes! So, we need to figure out how to bring creation along with us. We are Ministers of Reconciliation that God is using to reconcile the world back to Himself. He first reconciled us, now we must bring reconciliation to the world as well as to humanity.

Declare it with me "I am a Minister of Reconciliation; God is Reconciling the world back to himself through me!" Now say that a few times until you feel it, until it sticks in your mind and heart!!

When we are born again from above, we are then able to bring Heaven to earth. It's about getting righteousness into people through the born again process. It's also about getting the ideologies of satan and his nature off the face of this earth. We are to remove the leaders that follow satan out of the way, all these tyrants, these stains on the planet, removing them so that the land can be free.

The Bible talks about when the unrighteous are in charge, the people go into hiding, but when the righteous rule, the people rejoice. These evil ones are stains on the earth, and they're not supposed to be here, especially in positions of authority. It's time that we realize our positioning as Kings of God in the earth and tell them kindly to take a seat somewhere else.

As Kings of God, the way we free the earth, is we make sure to remove wickedness at the high places. But it's not a strain. We got to believe the right thing, understand our authority, and take positive unified action. We have got to believe that, "hey, hold on we're the Sons of God, we're supposed to manifest and set creation free!" Just by enough of us believing, there is a tremendous ripple effect. Our belief in the truth, and our knowledge of God's holy plan for this earth has the power to make the nations free!

But what's happened is so many people are believing that we're in this time of the Antichrist. People are living from the wrong age. And you can even see it right here. It says, Romans 8:22, we know the whole creation has been groaning as in the pains of childbirth until now. Creation has been groaning until now! We are here now as the sons of God! Now! There's no later date that we're waiting on to activate setting creation free; and I'm proving it to you guys in the scriptures, but also with my life.

I don't just talk about this; I live it out. God has blessed me with multiple lands, multiple houses, and we're multiplying animals, multiplying plants, multiplying seed, multiplying wealth, I have a giant seed collection, I give seed to those who ask. I'm growing thousands of fruit trees to make this world a better place. I'm growing all these sunflowers so that there are bees everywhere. There's a ripple effect to this you see! *What if we all were doing something like this??* I am multiplying life and bringing forth abundance. I am working to be a blessing to the Nations. You can't tell me that this belief bears bad fruit. What about the rapture belief? What about the end times (end of the planet) belief? What type of fruit does that bring forth? Not good! Judge a tree by its fruit.

Restoring the earth is our job description, we're Ministers of Reconciliation. We're rebuilding, renewing, restoring the broken places. It's not just people, see, we made this thing too easy. We're trying to make it easy because many are lazy, right? Not you guys, but the Church has been in many cases when it comes to teaching the fullness of God's plan. When I say "Hey, we're supposed to possess and rebuild cities," many have told me "Cory calm down, you're talking about taking over cities, what is wrong with you?"

Okay, well, if we don't take over cities, as the people of God, who does that leave in charge of cities? That leaves in charge the devil, we don't want the devil in charge of anything. We as the body of Christ are supposed to so fill this earth with the Glory and Knowledge of God, that satan's nature cannot even manifest, and that day will come. This earth was not made to manifest that unfortunate evil nature. We manifest the divine nature of God while cutting off the wicked nature of evil in the land. Declare it with me, ***I manifest the divine nature of God while cutting off the wicked nature of evil in the land.***

One time God spoke very clearly to me in regard to the Church. He said, "The job of the Church is to make sure the nature of satan never manifests on the earth again."

So, let's go to Isaiah 61. Isaiah 61 lays this out for us quite clearly, I will highlight some of the keys,

> Isaiah 61:1-9 The Spirit of the Lord God is upon me, because the Lord has anointed me to bring good news to the poor; He has sent me to bind up the brokenhearted, to proclaim liberty to the captives, and the opening of the prison to those who are bound; to proclaim the year of the Lord's favor, and the day of vengeance of our God; to comfort all who mourn; to grant to those who mourn in Zion— to give them a beautiful headdress instead of ashes, the oil of gladness instead of mourning, the garment of praise instead of a faint spirit; that they may be called oaks of righteousness, the planting of the Lord, that He may be glorified (for the display of His splendor).

They shall build up the ancient ruins; they shall raise up the former devastations; they shall repair the ruined cities, the devastations of many generations.

Strangers shall stand and tend your flocks; foreigners shall be your plowmen and vinedressers; but you shall be called the priests of the Lord; they shall speak of you as the ministers of our God: you shall eat the wealth of the nations, and in their glory you shall boast. Instead of your shame there shall be a double portion; instead of dishonor they shall rejoice in their lot; **therefore, in their land they shall possess a double portion; they shall have everlasting joy.**

For I the Lord love justice; I hate robbery and wrong; I will faithfully give them their recompense, **and I will make an everlasting covenant with them. Their offspring shall be known among the nations, and their descendants in the midst of the peoples; all who see them shall acknowledge them, that they are an offspring the Lord has blessed.**

See these first few verses speak about Jesus's assignment, right? Jesus came "to bestow on them a crown of beauty instead of ashes, the oil of gladness instead of mourning, and a garment of praise instead of a spirit of despair" right? That was what happened when Jesus came through in His ministry, He gave people salvation, He gave people hope and took away despair. Then this next part of this chapter is talking about **US** who received Jesus, **US** who would go on desiring to do the will of the Father. This next part in the chapter we can see expounds upon **OUR** job description as "Ministers of Reconciliation."

I want you to rightly divide this chapter. The first part is talking about what Jesus was to fulfill on the earth. "The scriptures are fulfilled in your hearing," He said in the synagogue when He began to preach this portion, but He stopped mid statement! It's because then after the part of Jesus, it gets to the part of US, YOU AND ME… DIRECT PROPHECY, FOR US who have received this praise instead of despair, this oil of gladness, this light instead of darkness, this freedom instead of bondage.

You must understand clearly that Isaiah 61 when it starts to say "They" it is talking directly to us who are in Christ!" You get it, got it?? Good!!! Let's go!

Then it says, "they will be called oaks of righteousness." "They will be called" - you will be called, you are an oak of righteousness, a planting of the Lord for the display of His splendor / glory! Wow what a powerful statement.. I have preached just this verse many times. So much glory in this verse. What does it look like to "display His splendor / glory?"

If you want to display His splendor, you have to start realizing that's what you're here for. Oh my goodness. See, he does all this. "They will be called oaks of righteousness." By the way, an oak tree is one of the hardest trees on the planet to chop down. You ever chopped an oak tree before?! An oak of righteousness, a planting of the Lord to display His Splendor Hallelujah!!

And that word "splendor" also means "richness, glory, and majesty." You're here to display the richness, glory, majesty, and splendor of Jehovah. You display His image, His richness. Come on!!! Believe this verse with me and watch what happens.

Say this prayer "Father God, let me display your splendor in this earth as an oak of righteousness!" The manifestation of that prayer crushes all kinds of problems and difficulties. Now say "I am an oak of righteousness, a planting of the Lord for the display of His splendor!!! Take on that as part of your Kingly Identity! Splendor, richness, majesty, and glory!!

Look closely here, it says in verse four, <u>they will</u> rebuild the ancient ruins and restore the places long devastated, they will renew the ruined cities that have been devastated for generations. Aliens will shepherd your flocks. Foreigners will work your fields and vineyards and you will be called priests of the Lord. You will be named ministers of our God. You will feed on the wealth of the nations and in their riches you will boast.

Who are these verses talking to? Think about this, meditate for a second! Yup that's right. It's talking to us right there; it's talking to you my brothers and sisters!! That's prophecy for us, 100% can't get around it, it is our commission in Christ! It's our calling. That's what Ministers of Reconciliation do. Get it? That's our job description.

Now it's time we think again about what we are doing personally with God, and how we can work together as the Body of Christ. We're supposed to be taking Dominion, oh goodness! When we got reconciled back into the Garden, we got reconciled back into that divine positioning of favor, but also of the divine positioning of blessing; the "blessing to be blessed, and to be a blessing." Remember, God spoke that over Adam and Eve!? We have the "Blessing and Dominion" "over all the earth" now restored and re-activated!!!

So that's why Jesus came to bring the Kingdom. He came to activate back the Dominion and Blessing so that the rightful heirs would take control of the planet and the meek will inherit the earth. We've been reconciled and, sin is removed, so now let's take possession of our inheritance, we take the title deeds to our lands in the earth in Jesus name! Now that the Kingdom is alive and activated in us, we carry the responsibility over the planet to become the divine stewards, the divine managers of the planet. We are rebuilding and setting the planet free from corruption while making known the manifold wisdom of God to the rulers and leaders in the high places. Why? Because they don't know the Kingdom Message either.

Ephesians 3:10-11 **so that through the church the manifold wisdom of God might now be made known to the rulers and authorities in the heavenly places.** This was according to the eternal purpose that he has realized in Christ Jesus our Lord,

Ephesians 1:9-10 **God has now revealed to us his mysterious will** regarding Christ—which is to fulfill His own good plan. And this is the plan: **At the right time (culmination of the age) he will bring everything together under the authority of Christ —everything in heaven and on earth.**

The Church is supposed to make known to the rulers in the high places this wisdom of God; that they're not supposed to be there anymore, this is our earth. It belongs to those who worship and obey the Lord! It's our job as the Church, and the Church is the Government of God not a religious organization. The Church is the Body of Christ as a Heavenly governmental body to rule and reign.

But brothers and sisters, the part that the Church has missed is that God put man in a Garden. And people are not realizing that we're supposed to be gardening, farming, and producing as well; not just reigning as Kings sitting around making orders. We must get the whole picture. Some people may say, "Cory, you're just saying all this about farming and possessing lands because you're farming, and you got some lands."

The truth is, I got land and started farming because the Bible said that foreigners are going to work my fields and vineyards and that I will have a double portion in MY LAND! I do this because the Bible says so. I can't help but manifest what I truly believe.

As I am writing this, I smell the sweet aroma of my workers here at the farm burning and clearing off the brush from my glorious land allotted to me by Jehovah! And I'm not bragging, I am boasting! Isaiah

61:6 "and in their riches you will boast." However, I also want to farm and love it. You will love it too, it's what Kings of God do!

> Ecclesiastes 5:9 But this is gain for a land in every way: a king committed to cultivated fields.

People lately are talking about, "we have this great reset taking place," *(a global talking point in 2022 by different global organizations, and global bankers).* Well, you know what I think this "great reset" is about? I will tell you. **We have too many consumers and not enough producers. We have too many people eating food and not enough people producing it. Too many ungodly people thinking they can lead. This is all changing because the people are awakening and many are already Kingdom Awake!**

Could you name 10 people that produce food? I bet you could name 100 or maybe 1,000 that eat food, right? So, we're way off. And in the Church, how many Churches are teaching their people to plant and/or to farm? If we continue this trend what will our children eat? I know what mine will eat, what about yours?? GMO NANO-TECH PHARMA food?? Seriously? We must multi-task, crush evil, teach truth, rebuild, reign and plant! And there is good wealth to be produced from growing food with the

Blessing. See the evil ones have to modify their plants to become synthetic because they have only the curse to deal with when planting real seeds.
We are to remove the powers of wickedness in the Heavenly places as well as over our cities; and as we do the Glory invades making life much easier for everyone around! I imagine we'll start understanding immortality more as we remove these enemies of God plaguing society. Remember Adam wasn't supposed to die; but let's not get off course. We first must do what God says to do, and in that order. He says the last enemy to be defeated is death.

Yes, it's easier to just talk about immortality rather than removing the demoniacs in the offices of authority. Who of you would take mission trips with me to the Governor's offices to pray and cast devils out? I'm sure some of you guys would. I've been saying that for years. Many of us have cast demons out at the street level, but it'd be cooler to see a devil cast out of a Mayor, Governor, or even a President, right?! We have power over all the demons, not just some; there is no difference, no "higher level higher devil." That statement is a lie. They have all been judged and now is actually their end time on the planet.

Matthew 28:18-20 **Jesus came and told his disciples, "I have been given all authority in heaven and on earth.** Therefore, go and make disciples of all the nations, baptizing them in the name of the Father and the Son and the Holy Spirit. Teach these new disciples to obey all the commands I have given you. And be sure of this: I am with you <u>always</u>, even to the end of the age.

Alright, read this next scripture,

Acts 3:17-25 "Friends, I realize that what you and your leaders did to Jesus was done in ignorance. But God was fulfilling what all the prophets had foretold about the Messiah—that He must suffer these things. Now repent of your sins and turn to God, so that your sins may be wiped away. Then times of refreshment will come from the presence of the Lord, and He will again send you Jesus, your appointed Messiah. **For He must remain in heaven until the time for the final restoration of all things, as God promised long ago through His holy prophets.** Moses said, 'The Lord your God will raise up for you a Prophet like me from among your own people. Listen carefully to everything he tells you.' Then Moses said, 'Anyone who will not listen to that Prophet will be completely cut off from God's people.'

"Starting with Samuel, every prophet spoke about what is happening today. You are the children of those prophets, and you are included in the covenant God promised to your ancestors. For God said to Abraham, 'Through your descendants all the nations on earth will be blessed.'

That's the gospel right there brother Peter! Great discourse!!! That's the message!! Peter is preaching, Guys repent, so that the anointing will come and your sins be wiped out, and you will receive times of refreshing, because all the prophets were prophesying about you people! That you would be the heirs of this promise that all nations would be blessed. **This is the promise of Abraham (which you will learn about in a coming chapter)**

Peter shared the condensed version of this promise, but if you go back to the promise, it was stated to Abraham that "your offspring would take possession of the gates of their enemies and all nations would be blessed." The gates are the supreme positions of power in the land. Okay, so this is saying, "Hey guys, repent! You're supposed to take over the supreme positions of power of the land, and through that all nations be blessed." That's the gospel family!!! The Message of the Kingdom.

What if we preached like this, "Hey everyone listen up. The prophets have all prophesied about this generation; those who repent and turn their hearts to the Lord Jesus will become heirs of the promise of Abraham, and that all nations will be blessed through you!! These prophets of old declared that you will take possession of the cities of your enemies and all nations and all families on earth will be blessed!!"

What if we preached like this? Well, we should be! Peter is announcing exactly what a new believer needs to hear when coming into the salvation of the Lord. Many of that time knew the promise God gave to Abraham, and they were waiting for it. Peter is telling them it is here and it is for them because Jesus Christ had made the way..

Today unfortunately most ministers don't know the Promise of Abraham or believe it already happened in the old testament. However, I will prove to you it did not. The past scripture should be proof enough, but we have more to come. The reason **many ministers can't accept this promise of all nations being blessed and God's people taking over the cities of our enemies is because it is contrary to their false end times belief of destruction**. We must remove views that are contrary to the Word of God, ESPECIALLY THE PROMISE OF ABRAHAM and Heaven invading this earth.

Galatians 3:13-14 Christ has redeemed us out of the curse of the law, having become a curse for us, (for it is written, Cursed [is] every one hanged upon a tree) **that the blessing of Abraham might come to the nations (Gentiles) in Christ Jesus, that we might receive the promise of the Spirit through faith.**

I would like to share something with you about this scripture. First, it says that Jesus was hung on a tree in order that we would have the Blessing and Promise of Abraham. Second, I want to clear something up; when it says, "that we might receive the promise of the Spirit through faith" that isn't referencing the baptism of the Holy Spirit, it is referencing the Promise that the Spirit of the Lord gave to Abraham in Genesis 22.

So, this Blessing and this Promise is very important to the New Testament believer. So why don't we hear about it? Well now we are. So pay close attention to what I am about to share with you!

I would like to prove to you who the seed of Abraham are. Who His descendants are.

Galatians 3:29 And if you are Christ's, **then you are Abraham's offspring, <u>heirs according to promise.</u>**

If you look into the NLT version, Romans 4 nails it. Paul simply shares the plan of God! Let's read,

Romans 4:13 **<u>Clearly, God's promise to give the whole earth to Abraham and his descendants</u>** was not based on his obedience to God's law, but on a right relationship with God that comes by faith.

To Paul it was clear. God's promise is to give the whole earth to the descendants of Abraham. And I just read to you; if you're in Christ, you're Abraham's descendants. That would mean this world is ours. Do you get what I'm saying? Once you get this message, this Kingdom message, you will begin to rise into your Kingship anointing and calling.

You all have to know that Jesus is greater than any wicked leader, any wicked system, and any wicked spirit. You have to know the promise of Abraham. You have to know Galatians 3:8 that says the gospel is that "all nations would be blessed." The Gospel is "all nations will be blessed."

Now, here's the deal. After I say all these things: all nations blessed, all thrones were created by and for the Lord and are for His people... you have to choose to believe it or it's not going to do anything. The Word of God is for us; receive it, believe it. The Word actually references us in the original language as "the believing ones." So let's get to believing the promises. Start by speaking! Faith speaks. Say, "I believe the promises of God, God's Promise and Blessing is for me!"

Good job!

I want to give an example of believing, because I am asking you to believe that all nations are about to be blessed, actually God is hoping you will believe that, rather than all of the doom and gloom – destruction-based doctrines. Now look at that verse in Isaiah 61 where it says foreigners will work your flocks and fields. I read that verse when I got out of prison and I was sleeping on someone's couch, and I had nothing. I read that verse and I said, "Well God, I don't know how that's gonna happen, but I will choose to believe it."

I choose to believe that I will have foreigners working my fields. And the wildest thing; as I am writing this to you I am out at my farm in Nicaragua looking out over the hills at my friends who are also foreigners to me because we are different nationalities, cleaning off my land and tending to my sheep and goats. God's Word is true! Just choose to believe!!!! All things are possible for those who believe. Believe all things are possible! Believe His Word.

I didn't know how that scripture was going play out, but I knew it was speaking to me so I chose to believe it. Choose to believe what God reveals to you in His Word. You don't have to have it all figured out to obey and believe. Think about Abraham, he chose to follow God and leave everything behind not knowing what was to come of his life. Let me say this one more time, the gospel is that all nations will be blessed, not destroyed, blessed!! We must paint this picture on the inside of ourselves.

Can you imagine all nations blessed with all rulers as the people of God and no more evil ones on the earth, but everyone knowing and being known by God!!?? This is where we are going as more and more of Heaven invades this earth. This is good news and we are just getting warmed up!!

Choose to believe the good news that we are the heirs of Abraham's Promise. We are the descendants of Abraham and by faith this promise is ours. We're taking back control of this world from the evil one. We have to make sure we renew our minds to the fact that we are reconciled and toil no more. We are living an abundant life. Now say this with me "I live life and life more abundantly!!"

We must realize we are Kings bought by the blood of Jesus, the Son of the Living God!! We are one with the Father, completely in His image and likeness, and if we believe for it, we will take over this world swiftly! We have all the backing of Heaven to do so, and I will continue to prove this to you. We must fix our minds on "taking over the world for Jesus."

If we will believe for it, all nations will be blessed! If we will believe for it all these thrones, powers and principalities of wickedness in the high places will fall, and we won't have to pick up a sword or a gun! **We can believe for it.** Speak for it, teach others, declare it, believe it some more, meditate on it, and by default, this thing will shift, and evil will fall until it is no more!!!

> Psalm 37:8-13 Refrain from anger and forsake wrath! Fret not yourself; it tends only to evil. For <u>the evildoers shall be cut off (seize to exist),</u> but those who wait for the Lord shall inherit the land. **In just a little while, the wicked will be no more; though you look carefully at his place, he will not be there. But the meek shall inherit the land and delight themselves**

in abundant peace. The wicked plots against the righteous and gnashes his teeth at him, **but the Lord laughs at the wicked for He sees that his day is coming.**

What a glorious passage to meditate. The power in seeing this vision that David saw!! Can you see it???! King David saw a world with no more evil and the righteous inheriting the land! Ask the Father to help you see this reality!

To close out this chapter let's read the following, and remember we are putting together the story of God; His plan for His Children and this earth. **You will begin to see this plan everywhere throughout the scriptures once you realize we are in the Eternal Kingdom Age. An age without end, an age where the Kings of God rise to take their positions over nations releasing blessing to all!**

Psalm 47 Come, everyone! Clap your hands! Shout to God with joyful praise! For the Lord Most High is awesome. He is the great King of all the earth. He subdues the nations before us, putting our enemies beneath our feet. He chose the Promised Land as our inheritance, the proud possession of Jacob's descendants, whom He loves.

God has ascended with a mighty shout. The Lord has ascended with trumpets blaring. Sing praises to God, sing praises; sing praises to our King, sing praises! **For God is the King over all the earth. Praise Him with a psalm. God reigns above the nations, sitting on His holy throne.**

The rulers of the world have gathered together with the people of the God of Abraham. For all the kings of the earth belong to God. He is highly honored everywhere.

A time is coming where the leaders of this world will be looking for the "people of the God of Abraham." We are the only ones qualified and appointed to lead the nations. We are the peacemakers, we are the ones with the Blessing and the Promise, we are the only ones who can trample the forces of evil. The people of the world will soon discover this, and demand God's people take their places of authority, our thrones in Jesus name.

The Kings of God are here!!! Say it with me **"The Kings of God are here!"** "And we are taking possession of our thrones in Jesus Name!"

Colossians 1:15-16 who is image of the invisible God, firstborn of all creation; because by Him were created all things, the things in the heavens and the things upon the earth, the visible and the invisible, **whether thrones, or lordships, or principalities, or authorities: all things have been created by Him <u>and for Him.</u>**

CH.3 THE ONLY END TIMES LEFT IS WHEN ALL OF HEAVEN INVADES EARTH

Alright brothers and sisters this is going to be an exciting chapter! Grab a pen and paper and write this at the top **"The only end times left you have to worry about is when all of Heaven invades the earth!" The eternal infusing with this earth!**

Now think about this, we pray Thy Kingdom come Thy will be done, on earth as it is in Heaven. Heaven is eternal, and as it invades, and as more and more glory invades this earthly realm, time will eventually become swallowed up with life! There will be no more need for time when all of Heaven invades this earth. We will live and walk in the realm of eternity!!!!

I had a dream one night where Jesus showed up to me and He said "the only end times you need to worry about is when all of Heaven invades this earth."

Now, I don't want to just be like "Whoa guys, Jesus told me this in a dream so let's go with it!" Jesus has only showed up to me 2 times in dreams that I can remember in my life. This being one of them. There was more to the dream but that is what He said. **"The only end times left you have to worry about is when all of Heaven invades this earth."**

First, I want to prove to you that the "End Times" spoken of in the Bible was actually talking about the *end of an age*, it was not talking about the end of the planet! You must must must get this if you want to understand the Kingdom Message. Many people are confused, they have these contradicting images inside of themselves. Just as I teach this you may be battling images you have inside of yourself.

Like when I say we will possess the land, you may have been taught theologies opposite of the meek inheriting the earth. Imagination is one of the most powerful creative forces on the planet when mixed with faith, we need to have it under our control! Our imagination should be in harmony with what God's imagination is for this earth and the future. We must put on the mind of Christ.

Let's do a quick declaration: "I am in charge of my imagination. My imagination works for me not against me. My imagination is full of the Truth of God. Any false visions or false images I command to be gone from me in the name of Jesus."

See, this is why tyrants use propaganda. Its why pharmaceutical companies use fear, they want you to imagine yourself sick, so that you get sick. What you carry in your imagination is extremely powerful. Many people don't consciously know what their imagination is doing, or what it is creating and believing for in the future.

We must have control of our imagination, not permitting external forces to hijack it. We must consciously paint the Kingdom Story / Message in our hearts. We must not imagine doom and gloom, nor the plans of the enemy coming to pass. We must imagine the will of God coming to pass and all of Heaven invading this earth..

> Matthew 6:9-10 Pray then like this: "Our Father in heaven, hallowed be your name. **Your kingdom come, Your will be done, on earth as it is in heaven.**

The question is, are we seeing this prayer completed on the inside of us?? You are supposed to believe your prayers, correct? Then let's start seeing all of Heaven and its will invading earth. And if Heaven is invading earth then, things must begin to get better and better, not worse and worse. How can things get worse and worse when we believe this prayer? Also,

Jesus wouldn't have taught us to pray like this if He didn't think we would get these results!!!

Now I want to teach you that we are not facing the end of the planet! This should be fun and liberating, believing for the end of the planet is super sad, kinda scary, and definitely unfruitful.

I'm going to go ahead and prove this to you today. Why is this so important? According to my estimate we have around 95% (in year 2022) of Evangelic Christianity believing we are still in the "last days", that is a pretty big problem. You do realize that for the past at least 100 - 200+ years they've been saying it's about time for the return of the Lord any day now, we're in the last hour. Many generations past have said this, they prophesied this, they wrote books about it. I had a book on my bookshelf someone gave to me called "The Window of the Lord's Return."

Well, the author missed it and all of the people believing this as well missed it. He probably made money off that book because as they say, "fear sells." It was a false writing, <u>bubbling up from ignorance as to which age we are actually living in,</u> and what the Return of the Lord was actually about.

Countless "prophets" have been incorrect about the Lord's Return, why? Because there has been a great misunderstanding that has taken place in the Word of God. But we're gonna go through the scriptures today, and you're gonna see for yourself.

First of all, let's go here to Isaiah 61. And we know that Jesus read this part of the scroll when He went into the synagogue and began to preach. But Jesus stopped in the middle of a verse and didn't complete it. Let's understand why.

> Isaiah 61:1-2 The Spirit of the Lord God is upon Me, because the Lord has anointed Me to bring good news to the poor; He has sent Me to bind up the brokenhearted, to proclaim liberty to the captives, and the opening of the prison to those who are bound; to proclaim the year of the Lord's favor,

And He stopped, right here in the middle of a sentence, "to proclaim the year of the Lord's favor." But the next part says, "**and** the day of vengeance of our God." So, we need to understand that he also came to bring vengeance. But it was not time to declare that just yet, remember His words carry much power. Jesus first needed to get to Jerusalem, His final earthly stop before being crowned King over the Nations upon arrival to Heaven!

Here is the deal, when believers in Christ are asked what they are doing, many will say they are waiting on the Lord's return. "Okay" I say, and then I ask them this question, you can try this out as well to see my point. I ask, "So what does that mean to you? What's Jesus going to do when He returns?" You will probably discover a different answer for every person you ask. You may also discern that most people telling you what is to happen at the return of Jesus are not actually confident in their story. They will say He is gonna do this or He is gonna do that, and when pressed they start making less and less sense. Some will admit they have no idea.

Let me share something with you, almost all the Prophets talked about this day of the Lord's return. And they spoke about it as a day of destruction upon the temple in Jerusalem, and the surrounding areas. A destruction that would take place when He returned in the clouds. It was the day of vengeance of our God.

The coming of the Lord, or the Return of the Lord in the clouds, was actually a day of destruction upon the enemies of God in the location of Jerusalem, the Temple, and the surrounding areas. I will point this out and prove this to you in the scriptures in this chapter! By the way this is good news so make sure to grasp this!

To start out understanding this "Day of the Lord's Vengeance" let's begin in Matthew 23 and read some of the "woes" Jesus declared over the teachers of the Law and the Pharisees.

Matthew 23:

vs 13 "But woe to you, Teachers of the Law and Pharisees, hypocrites! For you shut the kingdom of heaven in people's faces. For you neither enter yourselves nor allow those who would enter to go in."

vs 15 "Woe to you, Teachers of the Law and Pharisees, hypocrites! For you travel across sea and land to make a single proselyte, and when he becomes a proselyte, you make him twice as much a child of hell as yourselves."

vs 25 "Woe to you, Teachers of the Law and Pharisees, hypocrites! For you clean the outside of the cup and the plate, but inside they are full of greed and self-indulgence."

vs 27 "Woe to you, Teachers of the Law and Pharisees, hypocrites! For you are like whitewashed tombs, which outwardly appear beautiful, but within are full of dead people's bones and all uncleanness."

vs 28 "So you also outwardly appear righteous to others, but within you are full of hypocrisy and lawlessness."

So just to let you know, these Teachers of the Law and Pharisees were part of the target of God's wrath and vengeance described in Isaiah 61. In this chapter 23 Jesus is about to let them know.

Matthew 23:33 "Serpents, offspring of vipers, how should <u>ye</u> escape the judgment of hell? Therefore, behold, *I* send unto <u>you</u> prophets, and wise men, and scribes; and [some] of them <u>ye</u> will kill and crucify, and [some] of them <u>ye</u> will scourge in <u>your</u> synagogues, and will persecute from city to city; **so that all righteous blood shed upon the earth should come upon <u>*you*</u>,** from the blood of righteous Abel to the blood of Zacharias son of Barachias, whom <u>ye</u> slew between the temple and the altar. **Verily I say unto <u>you,</u> all these things shall come upon <u>this generation.</u>"**

Selah

In the previous scripture I underlined all the times it says "you" why did I do that? Well, it is very important now that <u>you</u> understand something called **"reader relevance"** this term means who is being spoken to in the context. What is the context? Not all passages are directly addressing us. Yes, we can learn from them but we must be aware of the audience Jesus is speaking to for many things to make sense.

It is clear from this chapter that Jesus is talking to the Teachers of the Law and the Pharisees. Correct?? He is not talking to you. Unless of course you are a snake and a brood of vipers, or a Teacher of the Law, or a Pharisee?? These woes are not addressed to the born again believer, rather Jesus is addressing the Pharisees and Teachers of the Law, **declaring a time of vengeance upon that generation.** Can you see that? If not, go read it one more time with the method applied of "**reader relevance.**"

This is important because we must understand that Jesus was dealing with a certain people who had become exceedingly corrupt, hindering God's people in the Temple and around the Jerusalem and Judea area. Jesus said to these "Teachers of the Law and Pharisees" in Jerusalem that all this bloodshed from the beginning, with righteous Abel on to Zechariah was going to come on **THEM** and in **THAT** generation. Hardly anyone will deny this truth.

When we use this same **"reader relevance"** method in Matthew 24 powerful truths are revealed. But many people will deny that Jesus is speaking to a specific audience about a specific time in Matthew 24. Why? Because they have a different imagination rooted in already and **"reader relevance"** methodology would rip it out.

Ripping out weeds from the heart may be uncomfortable, but when you do, the right beliefs can flourish. Plus, do you want weeds in your heart growing?? I know I don't and please help me if you see any coming up!! People must choose to humble themselves and be able to admit they're wrong to grow in Kingdom, and especially life abundantly!

Okay, now Jesus is talking about vengeance. This Matthew chapter 23 is where Jesus breaks into the vengeance discussion more. He is starting out with the Teachers of the Law and the Pharisees, and then directing his words towards the whole city of Jerusalem!!! But before we read this, I want you to take note of this:

A generation is 40 years, according to the Bible. Not thousands of years.

So, when we're interpreting the word "generation", It means 40 years, and it is wise to use the reference point of the Bible because we're reading the Bible. A lot of people try to use other reference points, but a generation according to God is 40 years. For example, He was mad at that generation for 40 years as they wandered in the wilderness complaining. That was a generation.

> Numbers 32:13 And the Lord's anger was kindled against Israel, and **He made them wander in the wilderness forty years, until all the generation** that had done evil in the sight of the Lord was gone.

So, Jesus is saying that all this bloodshed ("the day of vengeance of our God" from Isaiah 61:2) is going to come on that generation, this means within 40 years. So, what year do you think this was? This was right before Jesus went to the temple in Jerusalem. Right before the cross, so he was 33. Just keep that in mind. It was right around the year 33.

33 + 40 = 73 a.d. According to this prophecy of Jesus something significant should have happened on or before the year 73 a.d. in that generation.. And let me go ahead and tell you, SOMETHING SIGNIFICANT DID HAPPEN IN THE YEAR 70a.d. that every believer should be aware of. We will talk about this event in a moment.
Now, let's go to verse 37,

Matthew 23:37-39 **Jerusalem, Jerusalem,** [the city] that kills the prophets and stones those that are sent unto her, how often would I have gathered thy children as a hen gathers her chickens under her wings, and ye would not! **Behold, your house is left unto you desolate;** for I say unto you, Ye shall in no wise see me henceforth until ye say, Blessed [be] he that comes in the name of [the] Lord.

Jesus is now speaking to the whole city of Jerusalem. Jesus taught that you could speak to a mountain and believe in your heart that the words you say will come to pass and you'll have what you say. He is speaking to Jerusalem about something very important right now.

Jerusalem, Jerusalem, you who kill the prophets and stone those sent to you how often I have longed to gather your children together as a hen gathers her chicks under her wings, but you were not willing. **"Look, your house is left to you desolate."**

Okay, as you guys know, desolate would mean empty, barren, no one home. "Look, your house is left to you desolate," at this point I want to show you that Jerusalem was not desolate. Jesus was calling those things that be not as though they were, he was declaring the vengeance of our God upon

Jerusalem. You will see in the next chapter that Jerusalem was not yet desolate.

Okay, let's keep going,

> Matthew 24:1 **Jesus left the temple** and was going away, when His disciples came to point out to Him the buildings of the temple.

Now, this lets us know the location. We always want to know the context and location of where we are when we're reading. It is fun to know, it's important to know, it brings revelation when you know **where the dialogue is taking place, and who is talking to who.** Because just like I proved to you in Matthew 23, not all the chapters and verses are addressing us directly. Yes we reap from them always however we are not a brood of vipers, graves full of dead man's bones, whitewashed tombs. I hope you get what I am saying.

> Mathew 24:1-2 Jesus left the temple and was going away, **when His disciples came to point out to Him the buildings of the temple.** But He answered them, "You see all these, do you not? Truly, I say to you, **there will not be left <u>here</u> one stone upon another that will not be thrown down."**

Now most people quote this today, thinking that Jesus is talking about the planet. Not one stone on the planet will be left on another. However, they are talking about the Temple in Jerusalem and its surrounding buildings in this context, correct? It is clear to see when you think about context.

Jesus just told his disciples that all the buildings including the temple were to be destroyed! This is a pretty big statement that we must realize. He is telling his disciples that not one stone here, **(of the temple),** will be left on another, every one of them will be thrown down. Imagine hearing that from Jesus as you are walking through quite possibly the most religious area of the world, with the most beautiful temple of the world at that time.

Now the word "not one stone <u>here</u>" "<u>here</u>" "<u>here</u>" do you get it; it is talking about that location. Not the whole planet in some future Armageddon. **But countless Bible Teachers and believers do not make this correlation, they do not use reader relevance or read in context. They do not see that Jesus is talking about the destruction of the temple, so they have misinterpreted this portion of scripture and made a huge mess that we are now cleaning up, thanks to the Grace of God.**

Jesus was speaking in Mathew 23 and 24 and 25 about the day of Vengeance of our God to take place in <u>that generation</u> upon <u>that location</u>, to those enemies of God.

So, Cory, are you saying that millions of Christians have got this wrong? Thinking it is the end of the planet but actually this was talking about the end of the Temple Worship System, and the Age of the Law of Moses?!!

Yes, that is what I am saying. *Unfortunately, millions of Christians have not read Matthew 23, 24, and 25 in context or with reader relevance.* Strange and eerie actually. This is something we should have learned in spiritual elementary school.

This has caused them to interpret these scriptures as meaning the destruction of the entire world in the future, rather than realizing it was talking about the destruction of Jerusalem and the Temple, **and that Jesus was explaining to that generation the things they would see.**

Let's look at the next verses and then I will share,

Matthew 24:1-3 And Jesus went forth and went away from the temple, and his disciples came to [Him] to point out to Him the buildings of the temple. And He answering said to them, Do <u>ye</u>

not see all these things? Verily I say to <u>you,</u> Not a stone shall be left here upon a stone which shall not be thrown down. And as He was sitting upon the mount of Olives the <u>disciples came to Him privately,</u> saying, **Tell us, when shall these things be, and what is the sign of Thy coming and [the] end (completion) of the age?** *(not end of the world KJV)*

So next I am going to just review these verses with you and point out a few things. It says as **Jesus was sitting on the Mount of Olives, and the disciples came to Him privately,** "tell us" they said. When you are reading try to put yourself there in your imagination. Jesus was sitting on the Mount of Olives, the disciples came to him privately, and they were asking these three questions. When will this happen (destruction of the Temple and buildings), what will be the sign of your coming, and the end of the age??

So, it's interesting that they put those three things all together. Why did the disciples put those three questions together? Also, Jesus did not rebuke them for putting these three things together. When will this happen? What will be the sign of your coming, and the end of the age? Let me tell you why the disciples connected these three together.

The Disciples asked this three part question to Jesus **privately** on the **Mount of Olives (location)**, because the Prophets prophesied that there would be an ushering in of a Kingdom Age, a Kingdom of Righteousness. The Kingdom of God is an Eternal Kingdom that will continue to increase and cover the entire earth. Elevating God's people into positions of leadership over nations, and through them all nations blessed. But before this could happen it was also prophesied that God would make a new covenant with the people, meaning the old system had to be removed.

Now read Daniel 7:26 and 27. This is one of my favorite verses for sharing the Kingdom Message. It says,

> Daniel 7:26-27 "But then the court will pass judgment, and all his power will be taken away and completely destroyed. **Then** the sovereignty, power, and greatness **of all the kingdoms under heaven will be given to the Saints of the Most High. His kingdom will last forever, and all rulers will serve and obey Him."**

So, these disciples, who were students of the Word knew that there was going to be an end of that age they were living in. They knew that when the

Kingdom came, then there would be a new eternal age where God's Kings would reign on the earth.

They also knew from the Prophets that His "coming" was a day of destruction upon Jerusalem. They knew from Isaiah, Jeremiah, Zachariah, and many of the other Prophets. They knew that God had given chance after chance for His people in Jerusalem and the surrounding areas to repent, and they had not. You get it? That is why they're able to say "When will this happen, what will be the sign of your coming and the end of the age", because they knew the destruction of Jerusalem would usher in the next age (Aeon), **the Eternal Kingdom Age where God's Kings take over the world.**

No longer would the people have to operate under the Mosaic Sacrificial Offering Worship System based around a Temple. We now would become the Temple of the Living God! He would dwell fully in us! The destruction of the Temple in Jerusalem was the ushering in of the New Covenant.

Here are a few prophecies talking about Jerusalem and its judgment and destruction,

> Jeremiah 6:4-8 "Prepare war against her; arise, and let us attack at noon! Woe to us, for the day declines, for the shadows of

evening lengthen! Arise, and let us attack by night and destroy her palaces!" For thus says the Lord of hosts: **"Cut down her trees; cast up a siege mound against Jerusalem. This is the city that must be punished; there is nothing but oppression within her.** As a well keeps its water fresh, so she keeps fresh her evil; violence and destruction are heard within her; sickness and wounds are ever before me. **Be warned, O Jerusalem, lest I turn from you in disgust, lest I make you a desolation, an uninhabited land."**

Jeremiah 15:5-7 **"Who will feel sorry for you, Jerusalem?** Who will weep for you? Who will even bother to ask how you are? You have abandoned Me and turned your back on Me," says the Lord. "Therefore, I will raise My fist to destroy you. I am tired of always giving you another chance. I will winnow you like grain at the gates of your cities and take away the children you hold dear. **I will destroy My own people, because they refuse to change their evil ways.**

Amos 5:18-20 **Woe to you who desire the day of the Lord! Why would you have the day of the Lord? It is darkness, and not light,** as if a man fled from a lion, and a bear met him, or went into the house and leaned his hand against the wall, and a serpent bit him. Is not the day of the Lord darkness, and not light, and gloom with no brightness in it?

Zephaniah 1:12-17 **At that time I will search Jerusalem with lamps,** and I will punish the men who are complacent, those who say in their hearts, 'The Lord will not do good, nor will He do ill.' Their goods shall be plundered, and their houses laid waste. Though they build houses, they shall not inhabit them; though they plant vineyards, they shall not drink wine from them."

The great day of the Lord is near, near and hastening fast; the sound of the day of the Lord is bitter; the mighty man cries aloud there. A day of wrath is that day, a day of distress and anguish, a day of ruin and devastation, a day of darkness and gloom, a day of clouds and thick darkness, a day of trumpet blast and battle cry against the fortified cities and against the lofty battlements. I will bring distress on mankind, so that they shall walk like the blind, because they have sinned against the Lord; their blood shall be poured out like dust, and their flesh like dung.

Now you should be able to see clearly that the "Day of the Lord" was a day of destruction upon

Jerusalem. You can read the Prophets now and they will make much more sense and give depth to your revelation of God's heart and plan. Most people do not understand the Prophets because they don't understand that this Day of the Lord happened in 70 a.d. when the Roman armies besieged Jerusalem destroying the Temple, burning the buildings, and killing around 1.1 million Jews.

The Christians however escaped because in the chapter of Matthew 24, Jesus tells his disciples privately on the Mount of Olives the signs to be looking for when this "day of the Lord" and the "destruction of the Temple" and the "end of the age" were to take place.

Let's get back to Matthew 24.
The disciples privately on the Mount of Olives asked an important question. They asked Jesus, "When will all this happen, what will be the signs?"

Jesus began to tell them in the following verses, the signs that <u>they would see</u> before His coming, the destruction of Jerusalem, and the end of the age.

He shares the signs **they** would see; remember this is a private conversation on the Mount of Olives, we are just getting a sneak peek. **This is not talking about the signs you would see.** Jesus was warning His disciples **in that generation** how to avoid this terrible vengeance! And glory to God historians account (Josephus being one) that when they saw the armies surrounding Jerusalem, they fled to the mountains and were saved from that destruction.

Now I want you to take notice of how many times the word "you" is used, referencing His disciples. Remember **reader relevance**? The last chapter was speaking to Teachers of the Law and Pharisees. In this chapter Jesus is speaking privately to His disciples on the Mount of Olives, not you.

Matthew 24:4 And Jesus answered them, "See that no one leads **you** astray. For many will come in My name, saying, 'I am the Christ,' and they will lead many astray. And **you** will hear of wars and rumors of wars. See that **you** are not alarmed, for this must take place, but the end is not yet. For nation will rise against nation, and kingdom against kingdom, and there will be famines and earthquakes in various places. All these are but the beginning of the birth pains. "Then they will deliver **you** up to tribulation and put **you** to death, and **you** will be hated by all nations for My name's sake.

You will see this, you will see that, then you will be handed over. Jesus is clearly talking to his disciples; however many Churches are preaching this completely out of context saying that this chapter is talking about the destruction of the world, and these signs are for us 2000 years later.

I know partly how people got off track.

If you go to the King James Version, you will see that it says what will be the sign of the end of the world??! Rather than the end of the age (Aeon)!

End of the world???? UM WHAT!? So, the Greek word here is "aeon" which means "a Messianic time period or an age." It is not the word Kosmos which is used to reference the world. I have some ideas as to why it says, "end of the world." But regardless this is why we must be students of the Word. Now go check the Greek for yourself, everyone should have a study concordance.

This error has caused many ministers to put into our future, a day of destruction of the world, scaring families and in essence ruining the future of many. It's a crazy and seriously damaging theology, and one day many will probably need to humble themselves and repent for teaching this. I mean much of the Word is talking about restoring the world, i.e., God so loved this world He sent His one and only Son to save it not condemn it. God is reconciling the world back to Himself. I mean, you really have to eliminate tons of scripture to ascribe to the view that God is going to destroy the planet.

He did, however, destroy the Heavens, the Earth, and the Sea… Which is what they called the temple in Jerusalem. They called the temple the Heavens, the Earth, and the Sea because they created it to be a replica of the Kosmos. Did you know that? Most don't so they make this about the planet being destroyed when it was about the temple. We are now the temple of the Living God, and that temple in Jerusalem was destroyed in 70 a.d., within the generation Jesus said it would. Research this for yourself.

God is saving / "sozo'ing" the world. He had to destroy that Old Covenant. He had to destroy those Teachers of the Law and Pharisees, because they were exceedingly wicked, and He had to destroy the temple. People say why? Well ask Him. If you read in some of the Prophets, you will see that they were sacrificing children to demons in the Temple. So, God did not like the Pharisees and Teachers of the Law in Jerusalem. He had a problem with them and how they were living and oppressing His true worshipers.

Now after Jesus informs His disciples of the signs to watch out for before His coming, and the destruction, and the end of the age, He tells them a time frame of when all these things will happen.

> Matthew 24:34 Truly, I say to you, **this generation** will not pass away until **all these things take place.**

A generation according to the Bible is 40 years, remember? Well guess what, the temple in Jerusalem was destroyed in the year 70 a.d. That was 37 years after Jesus prophesied it. <u>That means all those things happened in that generation, and that includes His return.</u> Most people are still waiting on a return of Jesus. It happened already, at the time Jerusalem was destroyed!

People have said, Cory, are you saying Jesus returned already? Actually, Jesus said He would return in that generation. So, you don't have to believe me, you can believe what Jesus said! Some things prophesied in the Bible have already happened! That is good news. It would be a bad deal if **Jesus said all these things were gonna happen in <u>that Generation</u>**, and then they didn't. Get it?

"All these things" includes His return, go back and re-read for yourself. If you don't see it yet prayerfully ask the Father to help you see this chapter clearly. I understand that this is hard for people because they have had a picture that this return is some glorious day, when in actuality it was a day of vengeance upon Jerusalem and many of its inhabitants. Evaluate these scriptures for yourself, ask Holy Spirit to teach you and work to make your own conclusions with God. I am just showing you what I know.

Summary of this chapter: the end times the Bible speaks of already happened, Jesus already returned and brought about an end to the Mosaic Age; the age where believers had to offer sacrifices and worship God in the temple. Those days are over – end of an age. We are now in an Eternal Age, the ETERNAL KINGDOM AGE which is a never-ending age, where the increase of His Government and Peace there shall be no end!

An Eternal Kingdom that cannot be crushed and will cover the entire earth!!! With now a Church awakening to its Dominion and Authority to rule and reign, to remove and extinguish the rest of the residue of the evil one off the face of this earth!

An Eternal Kingdom is here, it is spreading "like a woman who puts a measure of yeast into three measures of dough, it works all the way through."

This is great news; you have a future that is bright! A future full of Heaven invading this earth. You just have to choose to believe that God's Kingdom is taking over and take positive steps towards a brighter future!

> John 4:21 Jesus replied, "Believe me, dear woman, the time is coming when it will no longer matter whether you worship the Father on this mountain or in Jerusalem.

"The only end times left to worry about, is when all of Heaven invades this earth." The light has come, and it will never stop increasing until God is in all and through all!

CH.4 UNDERSTANDING THE BLESSING & THE PROMISE OF ABRAHAM

In this chapter the conversation is going to be centered around **the promise of Abraham and the blessing of Abraham.** You must understand that these are two-fold. There is a promise that God gave to Abraham, which we will address. And there is a blessing that God gave to Abraham.

A promise, and a blessing. Get it? Two-fold!

God gave a really big promise with multiple statements contained in it to Abraham. We could say multiple promises, but it is referenced in the Word as "The Promise of Abraham." These are of supreme importance in the life of a believer, it is a theme or story-line woven throughout the Bible, and it's hardly ever taught in the Church, until now. The new believer when introduced to Jesus should also be introduced to the Blessing and the Promise of Abraham. Why? Well, it contains our purpose. Without revelation of purpose, we are wanderers.

Salvation is the what, the Blessing and the Promise of Abraham is the how and why!!

How many have ever heard the blessing of Abraham, or the promise of Abraham taught in the Church?? The "Word of Faith" people, they've heard of the blessing of Abraham, but in most other denominations and other churches you will hardly ever hear about the blessing of Abraham, and you will even more rarely hear about the promise of Abraham. Today with your help and understanding we can change this error, and help the Church realize the supreme importance of this blessing and promise in the life of believers.

Let's go ahead and start this off with prayer and a Psalm like we do here in Nicaragua.

"Father, in the name of Jesus, I bless everyone reading this message. I pray that this message would go far and wide, and that you would anoint this message so that people can receive your life and this blessing of Abraham, that they would understand the precious promise and be able to read with comprehension Father! And then as Kingdom leaders in this world we will make a supernaturally big and positive difference, in Jesus' name Amen."

Galatians 3:13-14 Christ has redeemed us out of the curse of the law, having become a curse for us, (for it is written, Cursed [is] every one hanged upon a tree,) **that the blessing of Abraham**

might come to the nations (Gentiles) in Christ Jesus, that we might receive the <u>promise</u> of the Spirit through faith.

Alright, so we're going to be in Psalm 144 and we're going to read the whole thing. It says,

Psalm 144: Praise the Lord, who is my rock. He trains my hands for war and gives my fingers skill for battle. He is my loving ally and my fortress, my tower of safety, my rescuer. He is my shield, and I take refuge in Him. He makes the nations submit to me.

O Lord, what are human beings that you should notice them, mere mortals that you should think about them? For they are like a breath of air; their days are like a passing shadow.

Open the heavens, Lord, and come down. Touch the mountains so they billow smoke. Hurl your lightning bolts and scatter your enemies! Shoot your arrows and confuse them! Reach down from heaven and rescue me; rescue me from deep waters, from the power of my enemies. Their mouths are full of lies; they swear to tell the truth, but they lie instead.

I will sing a new song to you, O God! I will sing your praises with a ten-stringed harp. For you grant victory to kings! You rescued your servant David from the fatal sword. Save me! Rescue me from the power of my enemies. Their mouths are full of lies; they swear to tell the truth, but they lie instead.

May our sons flourish in their youth like well-nurtured plants. May our daughters be like graceful pillars, carved to beautify a palace. May our barns be filled with crops of every kind. May the flocks in our fields multiply by the thousands, even tens of thousands, and may our oxen be loaded down with produce. May there be no enemy breaking through our walls, no going into captivity, no cries of alarm in our town squares. Yes, joyful are those who live like this! Joyful indeed are those whose God is the Lord.

Okay, so we're diving into the life of Abraham, because much of the New Testament is talking about Abraham and this promise and blessing of his.

Jesus was actually looking for sons of Abraham (those who have the faith of Abraham), most people don't know this. Jesus was looking for those who had the faith of Abraham. He was looking for those who had the faith of Who again?? Jesus was looking for those who had the faith of Abraham. I'm gonna prove that in a minute.

Not only was He looking for these people, He was also testing people to see if they had the faith of Abraham. So to start out, let's go ahead and go to the beginning. We're going to track through some scriptures, and we will let the scriptures tell the story. Yes, I just said "faith of Abraham" a bunch on purpose!! You will see why soon!

But before that, I want to put this in perspective for you. I want to share a brief story / testimony of mine. So, when I first encountered this blessing, I had not been taught about it, I didn't know what the blessing of Abraham was. There was no study on it that I ever went through that I remember.

However, one afternoon I got invited to this event with a friend of mine, the man who was mentoring me at the time. The event we were going to was called "Perspectives." I don't know all that they do, but apparently, they have people from different nations, missionaries, come and talk about the perspective of being a missionary on the field in that certain area. I had been invited there because I was about to go to Nicaragua as a full time missionary and live with my lovely new bride that I had met on my first mission trip. (One day you can hear that story if you ask!)

I remember getting invited to this event so clearly, and immediately I remembered hoping it didn't cost any money because I had like $0.00 in my possession. But I said, "Sure I will go. When I got to the front to pay not a supernatural thing happened except, they figured out I didn't have any money and my friend paid for me. Looking back, I know God honored my faith, even though nothing seemed to happen in that moment.

After all that front door access business, I walked through the doors! This event was being held at a beautiful Baptist Church that I had seen many times before in my high-school years. And the speaker for that night was a missionary from a country called Papua New Guinea. The man walked in the room and opened his Bible and said for us all to open as well to Genesis 12.

Let's go there now,

Genesis 12 Now the Lord said to Abram, "Go from your country and your kindred and your father's house to the land that I will show you. **And I will make of you a great nation, and I will bless you and make your name great, so that you will be a**

> blessing. I will bless those who bless you, and him who dishonors (or curses) you I will curse, and in you all the nations of the earth shall be blessed."

When this minister started reading, I began to feel the presence of the Lord, or of that Word extremely powerfully. I had already been baptized with the Holy Spirit about a year before that, and that was a raw power like, wow, you know, you know, when you get baptized with the Holy Ghost!!!

But as he is reading this passage in Genesis 12 I am feeling this Word entering me with raw Spiritual power just like the baptism of the Holy Ghost. It felt as if I was getting baptized with this Word he was speaking. "What is going on," I thought? And then I felt this Word just rest on me.

But I didn't know why. I didn't know why this man reading this blessing of Abraham had such an effect on my spirit. Why?! I am looking around at the other people in the event and it seems that this is happening only to me.

After that night I had to discover everything about this blessing of Abraham and why it is important for my life. Soon after I felt this Word rest on me I was surrounded by a new group of people, they were

Word of Faith Believers *(a unique group who have some powerful specific revelation on the power of Words, Faith and the Blessing of Abraham. However they didn't fully grasp and understand the Promise of Abraham due to "end times" contradictory views).*

I began hearing this group talking about and declaring the blessing of Abraham over each other, so I decided to hang out with them for a while and they mentored me. It was a glorious time of my life.

These men and women of God were about 30-40 years older than me and had been trained by Kenneth Copeland, Kenneth Hagin, Oral Roberts, and many other powerful men of God. These believers that God had brought into my life were very prosperous. Which was cool to see because I knew it was in the Bible. It was also cool to see that they were totally sold out traveling around the United States by hearing the voice of the Lord.

I actually got to meet the first two of them by going to an event God said to for me to go to one evening. I was inside and I heard God say to me "go outside" so I did. I saw two people, a man an his wife. We both looked at each other for like a minute knowing God was up to something. Then I said, "What are you guys doing?" They said "The Lord told us to come here to meet someone." Then they asked what

I was doing. I said, "Well the Lord told me to come outside and wait for something." And we were friends from that day on.

They were retired and we went to many healing revivals around the Midwest and saw many healings manifested. Cruising in my friend's old-school Jaguar car, it was a blast. He has since gone to be with the Lord (Brother Mike) but he imparted many things into my life that I am eternally grateful for.

However, to them this blessing of Abraham was used to obtain personal victory and prosperity, which is definitely part of it. I have since learned that this blessing carries so much more weight than personal victory and prosperity. In this chapter you will see much more of the power of this glorious blessing of Abraham!!

I didn't realize how important it was for us to get this blessing on our lives and flow in harmony with it. I don't think very many people on the planet in (2022) have yet to fully understand the implications of this blessing of Abraham on our lives. But by the help, and teaching, and confirmation of the Holy Spirit, I believe that this generation will rapidly learn what is on our lives in Christ!! Maybe when you finish reading this you can pass it on.

All right guys this is going to be powerful! So, the blessing of Abraham. Let's talk about it.

"Blessed are those who bless you and cursed are those who curse you!" We should say this a lot throughout our life throughout our day, because we need to have this mentality. A lot of people rise up in Christ and they think that people can curse them and have some effect, and they fear witchcraft, satanists, or others that may try and harm them. They think that people and satan can overcome them. But if you're believing the blessing of Abraham, you can't be overcome. Let me say that again, "If you are believing the blessing of Abraham, you can't be overcome!" There's no way to be overcome, but it must become yours and you must use it as a spiritual declaration / weapon and take it on as a mindset. We are more than conquerors through Christ who strengthens us!

"Blessed are those who bless you and cursed are those who curse you." So, anyone who comes at you with a bad intention, or even dishonors you is cursed, it falls back on them. Never rejoice about this, we want people to be saved and on our side. I have seen this happen to many people many times.

God has spoken this to me, He says "I raise up My people, and then they let their tongue destroy themselves." They say things like, "oh, man, they're gonna come after me for this one," or "oh man they might kill me for that," and on and on... Well, yup they just might if you speak it. Don't you know a man's whole course of life is guided by the tongue? However this isn't a book on the power of words, but if you don't use your words as a tool to work for you, you can expect a hard time.

I feel led to reference a teaching that greatly blessed me in regard to the power of words. It is a teaching taught by Andrew Wommack titled *"The Power of Faith Filled Words."* God really blessed me to find that teaching as one of my first series' I sat through.

What believers need to be declaring and believing as their foundation is this blessing of Abraham.

When someone begins to stand for Truth and Liberty and they begin to feel the pressure of tyrants, family, the law or whatever; the declaration should be **"Blessed are those who bless me and cursed or those who curse me." This helps to keep you in a posture of Kingdom (peace, joy, and righteousness in the Holy Ghost.)** When you really believe this Word, it shifts everything, and you stop having fear about everything. Stop here and meditate on that blessing for a moment, say it over yourself and ask God to make it real in your life, because yes, we are only touching the first part of this blessing. **This is a blessing of divine protection and divine prosperity. Blessed are those who bless you, cursed are those who curse you.**

Maybe it takes some time to start believing, but you need to believe it, and you need to know that it's predestined for the life of a believer in Jesus Christ.

Alright, so let's go ahead and read a scripture. Check out what Paul says <u>after the cross</u> of Jesus in the book of Galatians. It is key to wholeheartedly examine and meditate on this passage of scripture.

Galatians 3:13-14 Christ has redeemed us out of the curse of the law, having become a curse for us, (for it is written, Cursed [is] every one hanged upon a tree,) **[so] that the blessing of Abraham might come to the nations (Gentiles) in Christ Jesus, that we might receive the promise of the Spirit through faith.**

Jesus died on a cross; here says tree or pole. He died on a cross **so that... He died on a cross SO THAT** we would have the blessing of Abraham. If Jesus died on a cross <u>so that</u> we would have this

Blessing and Promise of Abraham, then it seems to me that this was not well understood by the Church.

If you were to ask 100 people why Jesus died on a cross, how many of that 100 do you think would say "Jesus died on a cross **so that we could have the Blessing that God gave to Abraham, and that by faith we would receive the Promise of the Spirit?**" Probably 0 out of 100 would say that. Why? Well, it hasn't been taught. And the implications of believing the fullness of this Blessing, especially the Promise would mean the destruction of mainstream doom and gloom theology. They would have to admit that God is restoring the earth, not destroying it. That God is blessing and rebuilding nations, not tearing them down.

Remember this is two-fold the blessing and the promise, we have not yet arrived at the promise. Nor have we heard all of the blessing!!!

Look back at that last part of Galatians 3:14 where it says, **"...that we might receive the promise of the Spirit through faith."** I must explain something here that is very important. Most people think that this means the promise is to receive the Holy Spirit, but that is not what this means. **It is referencing the Promise the Spirit of the Lord made to Abraham in Genesis 22. Again, this portion of scripture is

not talking about a promise to receive the Spirit, but rather to receive a Promise that the Spirit of the Lord made. We will get to this promise shortly.

Next, check this out,

> Galatians 3:29 **"And if you are Christ's, then you are Abraham's offspring, heirs according to promise."**

This is a huge scripture, say it with me, **this is a huge scripture!!** If we belong to Jesus, we are Abraham's seed, and heirs of the promise!!! And just wait until you hear this Promise!!!

Today in church we hear Jesus died on a cross so that you could have salvation. But do we hear that he died on a cross so that you could have a blessing, the blessing of Abraham? That all nations shall be blessed through you!!!?? "Blessed are those who bless you and cursed are those who curse you." Imagine how much confidence people would have if they knew that this blessing was on their lives from the beginning of their discipleship!!! Believe the blessing and be free!

Now declare with me **"I have the blessing of Abraham and I am free!"**

Here in Nicaragua I preached a message titled, "You have a blessing you don't know of." You have a blessing you don't know of. And you guys have a blessing that you need to know more about today. You need to know more about this blessing, how to loose this blessing because this blessing has spiritual power designed for the nations, impacting the globe, allowing you to release a global frequency.

This thing is not just a little goose bump like the average Christian craves. This is the blessing of Abraham. It is to transform the world; it is to bless all nations and families on earth! It is the Divine Word of power and promise to renew, rebuild, and restore everything the curse and satan have destroyed. Bringing Heaven and earth back into harmony and into the glorious freedom of the children of God!

> Romans 8:20-21 "For the creation was subjected to futility, not willingly, but because of Him who subjected it, **in hope that the creation itself will be set free from its bondage to corruption and obtain the freedom of the glory of the children of God."**

Jesus died on a cross so that the blessing would come to the Gentiles. Okay. But then it says **so that by faith, we might receive the promise of the**

Spirit. By faith, so this blessing is given to those who believe upon Jesus, however the Promise is by faith. What kind of faith you may ask? Well, we call it "the faith of Abraham."

The promise of Abraham is for God's Kings, for those who sincerely follow God and do His will. Abraham was told to leave his country, his father's house, and go to a land that the Lord would show him. And he did. Think about the disciples. He said "Follow Me," they had no idea really where they were going but they chose to obey. This is the "faith of Abraham," and this is the faith that enables the promise of Abraham to come alive in the believer's life.

> Romans 4:16 So <u>the promise is received by faith.</u> It is given as a free gift. And we are all certain to receive it, whether or not we live according to the law of Moses, <u>if we have faith like Abraham's.</u> **For Abraham is the father of all who believe.**

Now I have said in the past that Jesus was looking for the children of Abraham, those who have the faith of Abraham. Let me show you something you may have never realized until now which is in the story about Zacchaeus the tax collector:

Luke 19:8-10 Meanwhile, Zacchaeus stood before the Lord and said, "I will give half my wealth to the poor, Lord, and if I have cheated people on their taxes, I will give them back four times as much!" Jesus responded, **"Salvation has come to this home today, for <u>this man has shown himself to be a true son of Abraham.</u> For the Son of Man[a] came to seek and save those who are lost."**

Interesting right? Jesus was looking for the sons of Abraham. Why?? BECAUSE THEY HAVE A PROMISE THAT THEY KNOW NOT OF, A BLESSING THEY KNOW NOT OF. They are the ones who are the heirs of the promise that "all nations and all families on earth shall be blessed through!!" Glory!!!!

Ok now that I have built you up to see that there is a promise of supreme importance referenced all throughout the New Testament, it is time to read this promise that God gave to Abraham!!! Drum-roll wherever you are reading this!! Let's go to the famous chapter for all the wrong reasons Genesis 22! Why do I say for all the wrong reasons? Well, most preaching completely misses the point of this chapter, I believe you will see it today!

Genesis 22 (very important you read this chapter now, not skipping over anything you think you know already, every-time we read we can receive new revelation, read this like it was your first time.)

Genesis 22:1-18 Some time later, God tested Abraham's faith. "Abraham!" God called. "Yes," he replied. "Here I am."

"Take your son, your only son—yes, Isaac, whom you love so much—and go to the land of Moriah. Go and sacrifice him as a burnt offering on one of the mountains, which I will show you."

The next morning Abraham got up early. He saddled his donkey and took two of his servants with him, along with his son, Isaac. Then he chopped wood for a fire for a burnt offering and set out for the place God had told him about. On the third day of their journey, Abraham looked up and saw the place in the distance. "Stay here with the donkey," Abraham told the servants. "The boy and I will travel a little farther. We will worship there, and then we will come right back."

So, Abraham placed the wood for the burnt offering on Isaac's shoulders, while he himself carried the fire and the knife. As the two of them walked on together, Isaac turned to Abraham and said, "Father?"

"Yes, my son?" Abraham replied. "We have the fire and the wood," the boy said, "but where is the sheep for the burnt offering?"

"God will provide a sheep for the burnt offering, my son," Abraham answered. And they both walked on together.

When they arrived at the place where God had told him to go, Abraham built an altar and arranged the wood on it. Then he tied his son, Isaac, and laid him on the altar on top of the wood. And Abraham picked up the knife to kill his son as a sacrifice. At that moment the angel of the Lord called to him from heaven, "Abraham! Abraham!"

"Yes," Abraham replied. "Here I am!" "Don't lay a hand on the boy!" the angel said. "Do not hurt him in any way, for now I know that you truly fear God. You have not withheld from Me even your son, your only son."

Then Abraham looked up and saw a ram caught by its horns in a thicket. So he took the ram and sacrificed it as a burnt offering in place of his son. Abraham named the place Yahweh-Yireh (which means "the Lord will provide"). To this day, people still use that name as a proverb: "On the mountain of the Lord it will be provided."

Then the angel of the Lord called again to Abraham from heaven. **"This is what the Lord says: Because you have obeyed Me and have not withheld even your son, your only son, I swear by My own name that I will certainly bless you. I will multiply your descendants beyond number, like the stars in the sky and the sand on the seashore. <u>Your descendants will conquer the cities of their enemies. And through your descendants all the nations of the earth will be blessed</u>—all because you have obeyed Me."**

There it is!!! The Lord swore by his own self that He would multiply the descendants of Abraham (us in Christ, Galatians 3:29) as numerous as the sand in the seashore, also that His descendants will take possession of, or conquer the cities of their enemies, and through his offspring all nations on earth will be blessed, because he obeyed God!!!!!!!!!!!!!!!!!!!!!!!!!!!!!!!!

So, what do you think about that promise on your life in Christ?? Pretty big deal right? Also crushes the idea of things getting worse and worse when the Lord swore by His own self that all nations will be blessed! Why haven't we seen this take place yet??? Bad theology, people are believing for doom and gloom rather than "let your will be done on earth as it is in Heaven!" They are believing hell on earth, not heaven on earth. But this generation is awakening to the Kingdom Message and putting it into action!

I heard someone the other day say that "the Church is currently eating the fruit of their false beliefs and declarations." Stop believing for doom and gloom!! Heaven is invading and it isn't stopping until all the earth is reconciled back to God and God is in all and through all once again.

Ok, let's look at that promise again in case you missed it, "I will surely bless you and make your descendants as numerous as the stars in the sky, and as the sand on the sea shore, your descendants will take possession of, or (conquer) the cities (or gates) of their enemies."

Okay. This word **cities of our enemies** in the Hebrew is actually the word **gates of our enemies.** The word gate back in that time signified a place where the judges met, at the gate of the city, the judicial branch. It was the place where the people of supreme power met to make governing decisions for their cities and surrounding territories.
So when this promise says cities, it is not just referencing taking over cities. We are taking from our enemies, the highest positions of power in the earth,

and through this promise all nations on earth will be blessed.

Once we in Christ learn and stand up to take possession of these gates (positions of supreme power, or thrones), then all nations on earth will be blessed. God is just needing a little bit more faith than we have been using. And we are still looking for this to happen; all nations on earth blessed, and all nations led by the people of God. This is the gospel, "all nations on earth will be blessed!" And it happens through the descendants of Abraham taking possession, taking leadership of the supreme positions of power in the earth, and reigning as the Kings and Priests of God they are.

Galatians 3:6-9 In the same way, "Abraham believed God, and God counted him as righteous because of his faith." **The real children of Abraham, then, are those who put their faith in God.**

What's more, the Scriptures looked forward to this time when God would make the Gentiles right in His sight because of their faith. God proclaimed this good news to Abraham long ago when He said, "All nations will be blessed through you." So, all who put their faith in Christ

share the same blessing Abraham received because of his faith.

Now, I just proved to you, that if you belong to Christ, you are Abraham's seed, and heirs according to the promise. What's the promise?

Genesis 22:16-19 "And the Angel of Jehovah called to Abraham from the heavens a second time, and said, By myself I swear, saith Jehovah, that, because thou hast done this, and hast not withheld thy son, thine only [son], I will richly bless thee, **and greatly multiply thy seed, as the stars of heaven, and as the sand that is on the sea-shore; and thy seed shall possess the gate of his enemies; and in thy seed shall all the nations of the earth bless themselves, because thou hast hearkened to My voice.**

Get it yet?? You should burn this passage and promise into your heart, maybe memorizing it would be a good start! But when you memorize it, it is so you understand it, not so you can just repeat it. I usually don't tell people to memorize but rather understand, but in this case, you need to know the promise on your life, and you need to be asking God about it. He promised this to us who are in Christ, and I will prove it to you!!!!

Galatians 3:13-14 Christ has redeemed us out of the curse of the law, having become a curse for us, (for it is written, Cursed [is] every one hanged upon a tree,) **so that the blessing of Abraham might come to the nations (Gentiles) in Christ Jesus**, that we might receive the promise of the Spirit through faith.

Now new things that probably never made sense before in the Word of God, are going to make sense to you.

Let's go to Luke 19. You all probably know the story of Zacchaeus the tax collector, right?? Well let's read this one more time.

Luke 19:1-10 He entered Jericho and was passing through. And behold, there was a man named Zacchaeus. He was a chief tax collector and was rich. And he was seeking to see who Jesus was, but on account of the crowd he could not, because he was small in stature. So he ran on ahead and climbed up into a sycamore tree to see him, for He was about to pass that way. And when Jesus came to the place, he looked up and said to him, "Zacchaeus, hurry and come down, for I must stay at your house today." So he hurried and came down and received him joyfully. And when they saw it, they all grumbled, "He has gone in to be the guest of a man who is a sinner." And Zacchaeus stood and said to the Lord, "Behold, Lord, the half of my goods I give to the poor. And if I have defrauded anyone of anything, I restore it fourfold." And Jesus said to him, **"Today salvation has come to this house, since <u>he also is a son of Abraham.</u> For the Son of Man came to seek and to save the lost."**

So what was lost was the sons of Abraham, the sons of Abraham are those who have the faith of Abraham. They were lost because they had no direction with their faith. They had no purpose. They had nothing to do really, they were waiting on a savior, they were waiting on the reconciliation of all things. They're waiting to be reconciled. They're waiting for the planet to be reconciled. They were waiting on the Kingdom of God to come!

And Jesus said that Zacchaeus is a son of Abraham. Why? Because he demonstrated a great measure of faith. He climbed up into a tree just to get a look at the Son of God, he believed that Jesus was who they had been waiting for. This is a son of Abraham.

Okay. Now let's go back to the Word here.

We're going to look down a bit farther now in the same chapter Luke 19 and talk about the parable of the 10 minas, actually, let's look at the NLT version really quick.

> Luke 19:11 (NLT) The crowd was listening to everything Jesus said. And because He was nearing Jerusalem, **He told them a story to correct the impression that the Kingdom of God would begin right away.**

All right, you get that? He told them a story to correct their impression about the Kingdom of God. They had the wrong impression of the Kingdom of God; this story is to correct it. So, what did he say in the story? This story is extremely important because it explains how the Kingdom of God manifests. We must grasp this as the body of Christ.

> Luke 19:12 He said therefore, "A nobleman went into a far country to receive for himself a kingdom and then return. Calling ten of his servants, he gave them ten minas, and said to them, 'Engage in business until I come.' But his citizens hated him and sent a delegation after him, saying, 'We do not want this man to reign over us.' **When he returned, having received the kingdom,** he ordered these servants to whom he had given the money to be called to him, that he might know what they had gained by doing business. The first came before him, saying,

'Lord, your mina has made ten minas more.' And he said to him, **'Well done, good servant! Because you have been faithful in a very little, you shall have authority over ten cities.'**

WHAT!!! Because this steward managed money well and multiplied it, "take authority of 10 cities!!!?" Very interesting. Remember this is Jesus teaching the crowd how the Kingdom was to manifest.

Faithful stewards, taking charge, taking dominion of cities!! Cities! Cities! Cities! Sounding familiar?!! Promise of Abraham, wise stewardship, receiving dominion / Kingdom Governmental Official!! "And the government shall be on His shoulders."

Usually in today's preaching they leave out the "city" part, right? And just talk about being a good or bad steward. Again, possessing cities and making the world a better place has not been taught much yet. The Church has been stuck in the past ages, waiting on the end times which already happened.

But now, tens of thousands, maybe even hundreds of thousands, of believers are coming out of the religious trance and realizing our positioning as Kings that reign over the earth! This is why the enemy is so stressed and freaked out. He knows his game is over.

See, they had the misconception that the Kingdom was going to appear at once, so Jesus decided to tell this story of stewardship. And that those who could multiply for the Lord could be trustworthy to take charge, take dominion, have dominion over cities.

And then the next one came 'Sir, your mina has earned five more" his master answered, "you take charge of five cities." City, city, cities, okay.. Just like we read in the promise of Abraham, your descendants shall take possession of the <u>cities of their enemies</u> and through them all nations shall be blessed.

This tells us that we're supposed to take charge of cities. That's how the Kingdom manifests. We have been using our faith as believers for little bitty things. Things like going out on the streets, laying hands, opening blind eyes, those are good, and that's definitely a big deal to a natural person.

But a big deal would be removing a principality or power of wickedness in your city or state's leadership. Taking that position over, blessing and freeing the city, state, or nation! One thing I have learned in business is, if we can think big, we can believe big, and thus achieve big. Anything is possible for those who believe!!

Okay, we will talk more about this shortly. However, I want to connect you to this promise some more. Jesus is bringing up this promise. Jesus is talking about this conversation that God had with Abraham. "You too, are a son of Abraham, the Son of Man came seeking that which was lost." He was looking for those who had faith, the faith of Abraham. What was the faith of Abraham? Well, He left everything behind to follow the voice of God into unknown territory. He surrendered His will to do the will of the Father! The same thing Jesus asked of His disciples.

There are lots of people that have done this in the body of Christ today. Maybe you have laid down your will to do the will of the Father. **See, many people currently have this promise by faith spoken over their lives, but they throw it off with their words and end world theologies. If it's the end of the world then why bother taking charge of cities, right??**

But if it isn't the end and we begin to see that God so loved this world He sent His son to save it, then we have work to do. We must realize the Church has been lied to, and many drank it up. The "waiting gospel" is easy though. It takes no real faith and lazy people love it. It takes real faith to walk out and manifest Kingship on the earth.

Thy Kingdom come, Thy will be done on the earth as it is in Heaven. Let me ask you something. Do you think there are wicked leaders in Heaven? No of course not, because satan has already fallen and been judged. We need to manifest true Kingdom leadership, true Kingdom Government here on the earth as it is in Heaven.

John 16:11 "of judgment, **because the ruler of this world is judged."**

We need to see ourselves big and victorious with a promise from the Lord, and we must envision the body of Christ taking back everything from the defeated judged devil and his followers! Amen!

I have been teaching this message for around 10 years, and throughout these 10 years I have sat and taught many leaders what I just taught you. They understood it, they grasped that God's promise to us in Christ is to take possession of the gates (positions of supreme power) from our enemies and all nations shall be blessed. They have learned that the devil is judged. However, I discovered that many will not preach or teach this because they're still afraid of the devil. They don't want to talk about removing wickedness in the high places. They want to back pedal and teach other stuff.

Guys this is the Message, this is the Gospel, no more fear. **All nations shall be blessed because God's people take over the positions of power and lead the nations as Kingly examples of the Father.** Simple. You might want to re-read this and pause to meditate.

Today I have even seen ministers go as far as trying to teach that satan is just your ego, a figment of your imagination. Wow, that is a great help to the wrong kingdom. Teach people the devil doesn't exist, that is what he tries to teach people. You must to try really hard to believe that, but people do because they don't want to face reality, they don't read their Word, or they don't want to actually do what the Word says. They think it is too hard. When in reality, the victory has already been paid for and the enemy has already been judged.

The creation is just waiting on the Sons of God (not Son singular) to step up, manifest, and take responsibility. Making disciples of nations!! Teaching whole nations this truth you are reading now. The simplicity of the Kingdom Message. This is the truth that sets nations free!! You will see. "All nations shall be blessed" Galatians 3:8.

But it's easier to not take responsibility, thinks the lazy man, when in reality being lazy makes for the harder path, a selfish path that doesn't consider the generations to come.

They don't want to address this wickedness because they think it will magnify in their lives. Saying things like "don't talk about the devil or he will get bigger in your life." Seriously??! Only if you don't know the truth of his defeat! Why don't you try teaching people about his judgment (John 16:11), and our power to take back cities from our enemies? You will watch him get smaller and smaller trampled under your feet. Stop backpedaling those of you who already know the Kingdom Message. Use your faith in God, His Word, and His Promise!

> Luke 10:17-19 The seventy-two returned with joy, saying, "Lord, even the demons are subject to us in your name!" And He said to them, "I saw Satan fall like lightning from heaven. **Behold, I have given you authority to tread on serpents and scorpions, and over all the power of the enemy, <u>and nothing shall hurt you.</u>**

Choose to believe this Word and you won't have to be afraid of satan and the demons magnifying, you will realize they are subject to us, defeated, and we have authority to trample and overcome all the power of the enemy and nothing will harm you. Stop being afraid Sons and Daughters of God! We have work to do.

This is why we have to be the people that understand the devil is judged, and we have to let others know this as well. John 16 even teaches that when the Holy Spirit comes, he will convict the world of three areas, one of them being the fact that the devil has already been judged. (Read John 16:11)

See we in Christ, the "Believing Ones" with Jesus as our King and Lord, who seek to do the Will of the Father, have supreme power in this earth, not satanists, not witches, and definitely not the devils. If satanists really knew what satan had planned for them (to suck them dry and kill them, dragging them to the place of torment with him) they would all repent quickly and join the side of truth, regardless of all the idle threats of his organizations.

As a matter of fact, if you are reading this and are trapped on the wrong side, I declare you free in the name of Jesus. Now repent, ask Jesus to be your Lord, pick up your Bible and put what you read into practice.

We are the nation high above the nations of earth. All thrones were created by and for Jesus. And the time is now that we take over, but we must understand this. The more people that understand this message of takeover, and are believing this, the easier it is.

We are now hearing of active Pastors taking office because they see that God is not ok with wickedness in these positions. We need to be putting movement, and momentum to this, helping Kingdom leaders to take possession of what God has for them. A lot of them, God's already spoken this "well done my faithful steward, take charge of cities" over their lives. We just need leaders who are willing to erase the false rapture / end times fruitless demonic theologies from their hearts and realize God so loved this world!!! This world is ours; we are co-heirs with Jesus!

We must think bigger. We must realize that possessing a city is not hard. Being the leader of a city is not that hard. It's harder rather to be living in a city under a person, or group of people possessed by evil spirits trying to make rules for God's people to live under. This is not the way it is to be my brothers and sisters. God does not want this. We must take Kingdom, we must take Kingship and leadership of this planet. The world is looking for Godly leaders who walk in complete victory to step up and be the Kings and Priests we are called to be.

We must also realize that this is not about politics in any way, by the way. Politicians in this day have become basically actors. If you ever make this about only politics, you step down a level to where men start fighting you, yes with their egos lol. The Kingdom is higher than politics, we come from Heaven's Government. People who don't know God are no longer to be leaders of our world, declare this often in the name of Jesus!

Imagine if all the "Prophets" realized this and spoke in harmony with God's will for creation! It will happen. Share this book with your Prophet friend, I have found that they are about the most open crowd within the Church to hear.

See we talk about crushing the devil not people. We talk about satan tricking people in power, which is the root of many problems. You will find a lot less confrontation when exposing the devil over people. Why? Well he doesn't want the world to know he exists, and then find out he is judged and stripped of his authority, because then people repent and turn to Jesus.

Nobody really messes with me, first they would have to get through Jesus and my Angels, but then they would have to admit the devil is real and that they're following him. It's a higher way of attack, but I do believe there is a time for confronting those who host these devils willingly for their crimes, to bring them to justice (jails/prisons/psych-wards like others who commit crimes) and hopefully bring them to repentance.

Anyways we must remember that our war is not against flesh and blood, but against principalities, powers of wickedness in the high places, and we ought to get back to binding these evil spirits and commanding them to their place of torment. Remember, the devils who were worried Jesus came to torment them before their time??

Well now is their time of torment. Jesus has already ascended and been made King over the nations! We don't send these evil spirits into pigs anymore, or chihuahuas. We send them to their place of torment, the lake of fire.

John 12:31 "Now is [the] judgment of this world; **now shall the prince of this world be cast out**"

You don't need to fast more or pray more to cast out devils and walk in victory. You need to believe the TRUTH, and the truth is satan has been judged. We have the power and backing from heaven to remove these evil spirits from the high places, and from off the face of our earth. Remember "on earth as it is in Heaven." There is no devil in Heaven, so there shall be no devil on earth. Imagine that!!!!! Seriously imagine that often because that is what the future holds according to the Word and Will of God.

God wants His Kings reigning on the earth now, you just got to lay down your life, lay down your will to do the will of the Father, and it's a glorious plan!

Is it clear to you yet that God's promise was to give the whole earth to us?

> Matthew 5:5 Blessed are the meek, **for they shall inherit the earth.**

That's powerful, but have you read Acts 3 where Peter preaches to the crowd?? He totally nails a powerful example of how we should all present the Gospel to a new believer, even how we should re-present the Gospel to the Church in my opinion!

> Acts 3:19-25 Repent therefore and be converted, for the blotting out of your sins, so that times of refreshing may come from [the] presence of the Lord, and He may send Jesus Christ, who was foreordained for you, whom heaven indeed must receive till [the] times of [the] restoring of all things, of which God has spoken

by the mouth of His holy prophets since time began. Moses indeed said, A prophet shall [the] Lord your God raise up to you out of your brethren like me: Him shall ye hear in everything whatsoever He shall say to you. And it shall be that whatsoever soul shall not hear that prophet shall be destroyed from among the people.

And indeed, all the prophets from Samuel and those in succession after [him], as many as have spoken, have announced also these days. *Ye* (you all) are the sons of the prophets and of the covenant which God appointed to our fathers, saying to Abraham, and in thy seed shall all the nations of the earth be blessed.

You know, we have been taught all nations are going to be destroyed. That things are supposed to get worse and worse, all the while the Bible is saying the Gospel message is that "all nations shall be blessed", and that "My house shall be called a house of prayer for all nations!!" We've been taught a bunch of stuff to keep us from seeing the CLEAR PICTURE OF ALL NATIONS AND ALL FAMILIES BEING BLESSED!

This is the gospel: all nations being blessed by God's children who take possession of cities, even nations, and through them, all nations, all families on earth will be blessed!

Now preach it! How else will people hear and believe the good news!? The world has eaten a synthetic watered down GMO gospel. The Church needs a detox.

When we identify these people of Kingdom Government, we need to nudge them into place, encourage and help them, and let them do their jobs. That is what God has shown me. I keep hearing the Lord say, **"Let my Kings be Kings."** Because right now we got a bunch of impostors who don't know God trying to dictate the ways of life to humanity. Churches if you know one of these Kings of God, "faithful stewards" you need to nudge him or her into their office of Kingship, maybe first kindly nudge them to study this book with you.

Maybe start a Bible study with this book. The more groups of us actively working in the name of Jesus to take possession of this earth, the more we can all connect! Thus, we can work together as the Body of Christ on this objective of Heaven's Government invading and filling the earth. All of us Sons and Daughters of the Most High coming to the realization that the Children of God are commissioned to set creation free from its bondage to corruption. LET'S GET IT DONE!!!!!!!!

CH.5 UNDERSTANDING THE KINGDOM TAKEOVER MESSAGE

Today is an epic day in history, I can feel it through my bones! The Lord has been downloading to me so much, so much revelation on the history of our planet, and what the inhabitants have gone through to get to this point. God has spoken to me that this is a "generation of opportunity." It may not look like it right now, but it is, and we need to use our faith to see that the world is awakening to something so powerful.

I was listening to this man on a live stream today and he was giving an overview of the history of the world. I don't know who he was, but it was an excellent broadcast from Charis Bible College. I would love to find him again. Throughout the history of the world humanity has basically lived under kings, tyrants, dictators, etc. for 1000s and 1000s of years. Every once in a while, there was a good king, but then he would get greedy, and this or that would happen. Basically there were very few kings that were considered godly and righteous.

So, then the Bible got translated from the original languages into languages that people could actually read and carry for themselves, they could carry their own Bible. This was a big shift, because suddenly now believers could read the Living Word with God's will revealed! They started reading it, and they started realizing that they could have faith in this Word and see it come to pass.

Well, along came Martin Luther and he realized a bunch of things that were taught incorrectly. He realized that salvation came through grace, not by works like so many of that time were teaching and unjustly benefiting from.

We don't have to do all these works to get saved!! He brought out the revelation that salvation is by faith through grace, not by works. He realized some things that were massively wrong in his day, and consequently, he went against the grain and he took a stand. Then the people saw it for themselves as they studied the Word, and some of the believers of that time were able to step into a higher level of grace and understanding of God's heart and will.

We are in similar times my friend. We are realizing what has been in the Word of God all along, what the teachers have missed, "The Message of the Kingdom!" God's mysterious plan is now revealed (Ephesians 1:9-10)

So, then this Historian on the live stream starts explaining about this group of "pilgrims" that were going from place to place to be free. They ended up on a boat and arrived in the United States of America, and with no King over them!! There was no one in the land, except Indians. They had the Word of God and no king on that giant piece of land saying you must believe like me. In the past kingdoms had this idea that whatever religion that king had, you were supposed to believe the same. Now what were these pilgrims to do??

There is obviously so much more to this story, but the USA began its steps towards complete freedom and liberty from Great Britain. Forming a republic, the Republic of the United States of America, where the people have the power, where there's personal freedom and liberty, where we get to select our representatives, a more Biblical form of Government. Leadership in the Kingdom is a willingness to follow and not forced upon. One of the definitions of the word Liberty is "freedom from oppressive government."

Now, in the USA, there was something new that had never existed before on the planet that we know of. It was a government, of the people, by the people, for the people. An attempt at self-government via Christian principles and morals. It wasn't based on bloodline, royal families, and greedy tyrants. It wasn't any of that, it was something new. These people grew and became free, they fought wars against communism and all these different attacks, and they stayed free for hundreds of years.

Now, all of a sudden, the United States of America appears to the human eye to be on the verge of collapse. But not to the heart of God. Why? Why is this going on? Well in the message following in this chapter you will learn that the enemy knows his time is short so he is trying to take down as many as he can with him.

We've preached this before, but this time is different, this time satan knows. This message that we are about to talk about, is the message that the devil doesn't want out. The Kingdom Message is out though and growing like yeast in a batch of dough, working all the way through the earth!!

We have another Martin Luther moment happening right now where more revelation is occurring, except this time much broader. We are now understanding the story/plan, the purpose of God, and the heart of the Father. We see something in the Word of God which is ours, that we have not fully manifested yet, and we have been told by institutions, and organizations, that it's later or not yet just wait. Just wait. "Yes you are Kings, but not yet"?? Just wait…?

We are not waiting anymore!

We are seeing and learning that we are Kings of God right now! That we were purchased by the blood of Jesus to be Kings that reign on the earth now! We are believing it! We are demanding it, and the devil is freaking out. Why do you think they're trying to censor like never before? Why is the propaganda so strong (2021-2022?) Why are they trying to kill everybody all at once with all these different mechanisms of depopulation?

They're wearing themselves out, printing paper dollars, all the while their illusion, their fantasy is failing. **It's the fall and exposure of the evil empires in this world.** That is what the Kingdom Message manifests. The Eternal Kingdom is here that crushes and brings to nothing all other Kingdoms but it endures forever.

Daniel 2:44-45 **"During the reigns of those kings, the God of heaven will set up a kingdom that will never be destroyed or conquered. It will crush all these kingdoms into nothingness, and it will stand forever.** That is the meaning of the rock cut from the mountain, though not by human hands, that crushed to pieces the statue of iron, bronze, clay, silver, and gold. The great God was showing the king what will happen in the future. The dream is true, and its meaning is certain."

This is why we see lock-downs, pandemic scares, emergency powers, lock step, agenda 2030 but 9 years early. This is also why we see travel restrictions. Those who said no to God and hate the light and want to contain the Kingdom Message, but here I am up in my off-grid house way out in the middle of nowhere, under the starry night sky with 2 of dogs, me and the moon shining so bright, writing to you the truth that sets nations free, Glory!!

Now is the time of the Great Expansion of God's Kingdom, get ready! A Kingdom Teaching Revival!!

Two and a half years ago, when this all started (lock-downs, canceled flights, scary virus, etc), you know that I had a campaign plan to go all around the USA preaching the Kingdom Message, and I had my business producing quite well. I didn't need anybody to fund or donate anything to the ministry. I was going to host events, banquets, BBQ, music, and everything, while teaching this Kingdom Message with some others who had gained this revelation. To bring everyone into harmony with this message they were learning. We will persevere in this endeavor and make it happen in the name of the Lord Jesus!

I had a stack of money I had allocated for the Kingdom; I was going to use it to get the Kingdom Message out and connect everybody. We were going to have meetups all over the USA and potentially the world preaching the Kingdom Message. It was said to start right when the "plandemic" / flights canceled happened. I had bought 3 plane tickets, 3 different times, only to have them cancel and take my money. One said they had a credit but that is beside the point.

Now, I'm not saying that this is because of me. I am saying this because His Kingdom Message is being realized all around the world! **This revelation of the Kingdom Message is the Truth that sets nations free, and free from tyrants forever.** At the time of writing this my podcast has over 20k downloads, 55+ nations, and many more listeners. There have also been thousands through my Kingdom University (see resource section in the back of the book), and many are listening to the audio version of this book as I edit this version for print! People are hungry for this revelation, and they need it now.

There are many others who understand this message now, and they started speaking to others about the Kingdom Message, and a *"Godly Gossip"* if you will, started to spread. With the question "is it really time to take over the planet for Jesus?" **The answer is yes and this book more than proves it,** but this is why we see the devil completely exposing himself and his system, frantically trying to censor those who believe in Jesus. Why not before? Why all of a sudden is there a global demonic attack in plain sight?? Well, satan was ok with the Church's message that taught *wait*, because that message let him stay in power. This Kingdom Message removes him, and ushers in the Kings of God who worship and obey the Lord Jesus. The Kings of God that liberate creation from its bondage to corruption and decay, these Kings are now here!!!

We are not waiting anymore!

Now you need to read this next scripture closely, as this is one of the most important scriptures to get the clear picture of the Kingdom Message. Meditate on this one often.

> Daniel 7:26-27 **"But then the court will pass judgment, and all his power will be taken away and completely destroyed.** Then the sovereignty, power, and greatness of **all the kingdoms under heaven will be given to the holy people of the Most**

High. His kingdom will last forever, and all rulers will serve and obey Him."

Do you see it? Once the court sits, all kingdoms under heaven (which would be in the earth) will be given over to the people of the Most High, **and his Kingdom will last <u>forever</u> (key word)**, and <u>**all**</u> **rulers (key word)** will serve and obey Him.

You need to be able to meditate on this and make it your reality. This is proven all throughout the Bible but here it is concisely written **what will take place after** the Judgment of our enemy which we have proven has already happened, (John 16:11).

To give more evidence that this period of Kingdom Takeover is now, I would like to remind you of what Jesus said to his disciples after his resurrection, and before his ascension into his position of power at the right hand of the Father in Heaven.

Matthew 28:18-19 And Jesus came and said to them, **"All authority in heaven and on earth has been given to Me.** Go therefore and make disciples of all nations, baptizing them in[a] the name of the Father and of the Son and of the Holy Spirit"

There is much to say about these words, however I want to draw your attention to the fact that Jesus said, "All authority in heaven and on earth has been given to me." This means that the power of the devil has been taken away, and is being completely consumed until every trace of his nature on earth is wiped out.

BUT you must see that this is much bigger. Not only is Jesus saying all authority in Heaven and on earth is His, but He is also implying that we are at the time where all Kingdoms under the whole Heavens are to be handed over to the Saints, the people of the Most High God.

Let me share something else, to make sure you see this.

Isaiah 9:6-7 **For unto us a child is born, unto us a son is given; and the government shall be upon His shoulder;** and His name is called Wonderful, Counselor, Mighty God, Father of Eternity, Prince of Peace. **Of the increase of His government and of peace there shall be <u>no end,</u>** upon the throne of David and over his kingdom, to establish it, and to uphold it with judgment and with righteousness, **from henceforth even for ever.** The zeal of Jehovah of hosts will perform this.

If you meditate on this, which I hope you will take the time to do, with a calmness in your heart, and an inquiring of the Lord, you will see many powerful truths. First, when this child is born, this Son of God Jesus, the government will be on His shoulders. As soon as He was born He brought the Kingdom of God into the earth, the Government of God. Since His birth this Kingdom has been expanding and will continue to expand forever. It is an Eternal Kingdom, and it is here on earth now! We are in the Eternal Kingdom Age. Heaven is invading earth!

Are you getting this?? Jesus signified the end of satan's rule, this is why when He first sent out His disciples He said "repent for the Kingdom of God is at hand." Then He told them to go out and cast out devils, heal the sick, raise the dead, and declare the good news.

Why did He say cast out the devils?? Why did He say repent?? Well, there are many answers I am sure, however repent means change your way of thinking. Many think Jesus was only meaning turn from your sin and turn to God, which is part of it. But what if Jesus was saying repent, the Kingdom of God is here to finally crush satan's rule in the earth!!!??

I mean what were the people waiting for at that time, they were sitting in darkness, evil ruling the world, they were looking for deliverance from these evil spirits! Jesus brought this, and this is also why His disciples returned overjoyed saying even the demons are subject to us. And Jesus responded in a way worthy of meditating on, **"I saw satan fall like lightning from heaven."**

The enemy fell from his positioning, and he fell from Heaven. Jesus came to help empower us to be free Kings and remove him, and all traces of him, off the face of this earth!

1 John 3:8 **The reason** the Son of God appeared **was to destroy the works of the devil.**

This message I am telling you started spreading all throughout the USA, Canada, Australia, New Zealand, the Netherlands, and the UK, infecting in a good way, the world. We are reaching over 55 nations now. And so, these forces had to come up with a plan. They needed a distraction, they needed to show some muscle to throw people off and keep them from talking more about this, hahaha I am laughing as I write this. It's so game over for evil!

The evil ones, some call them globalist I call them satanists, did not know that this message would take hold so fast. They knew that I knew it and had been teaching it, but for the most part people were calling me false teacher, anti-Christ, and other things for many years. But then people began to listen, and others began to get the revelation, and we began to connect and communicate our revelations regarding the age we are now living in. The Eternal Kingdom Age as the Kings and Priests of God to rule and reign on earth!

These forces knew they couldn't stop me from getting this message out, thanks to God for His hand on my life, and they got scared. So, they wanted to cut communication (for example some phones, I won't say which ones, are using speech recognition to make sure my voice can't be heard on their devices and operating systems.) Which is why I knew I had to get this revelation out in print and around the world quickly. I hope that you will help.

They wanted to cut us off from gathering with each other because when we meet together with revelation of this message, and we talk about this message and pray for the nations, I'm telling you what, it is a whole different realm of anointing. **We call it the Kingdom vortex, when believers get together with this message and pray for the**

nations! Man, I experienced Heaven on earth in a powerful way in Fort Worth, Texas with some other powerfully anointed Men of God! One of the most glorious days of my life.

All right. That was a long introduction to this chapter, let's learn now the "Truth that sets Nations free." One time I asked God, "Father, I know that knowledge of the truth sets us free, but wouldn't it also be true that there is a knowledge of a truth that could set whole nations free???" He said "Yes, the Kingdom Message will set nations free, all nations shall be blessed."

In this chapter, I'm going to prove to you **what the Kingdom Message is.** You must know the Kingdom Message. You must also know how to keep it simple, break it down simple, and not wander off into fine sounding doctrines. "Heaven on earth, earth and man reconciled back to God." It is simple and glorious!

Now I need to warn you, I have seen many believers over the years get this Kingdom Message and then fall away to the wolves in sheep's clothing. They talk sweet, pretend to listen, acting like they are a friend, only to bring poisonous ideas and teachings to stop you from manifesting your Kingly authority now. *Pray for discernment, wisdom, and understanding.*

I have unfortunately seen more fall into false doctrines than I have seen who continue with the simplicity of the Gospel. Don't let this be you and don't let this discourage you. Trust me there is plenty of Glory, Splendor, Majesty, Prosperity, and Power in this simplicity! Pause and ask Holy Spirit to help you understand the Kingdom Message we are about to discuss and take notes.

Galatians 1:6-8 I am shocked that you are turning away so soon from God, who called you to Himself through the loving mercy of Christ. **You are following a different way that pretends to be the Good News but is not the Good News at all. You are being fooled by those who deliberately twist the truth concerning Christ.** Let God's curse fall on anyone, including us or even an angel from heaven, who preaches a different kind of Good News than the one we preached to you.

Keep it simple, you don't have to fall into the trap of being in the cool club or being the most spiritual talker in the group. We are not idolizing people. There is such power in the simplicity of this Message, enough to unite the whole world around the Kingdom of God. The Bible says to stay away from those who talk too much and can't listen. Make sure you are not one of those. I have this concept that has served me well; if a person can't state their view simply, it's because they don't really know what they are talking about.

> Matthew 13:18-19 "Now listen to the explanation of the parable about the farmer planting seeds: **The seed that fell on the footpath represents those who hear <u>the message about the Kingdom</u> and don't understand it.** Then the evil one comes and snatches away the seed that was planted in their hearts.

The parable of the Sower is about a farmer planting the Word of God, and there's all these different types of hearts, these different types of people, however there's only one type that produces fruit, only one type. Only the man or woman, who retains the Word of God with a noble heart, and through perseverance brings forth fruit.

Now you must understand from the previous scripture that the devil is coming after the **"Message of the Kingdom."** There's a lot of other messages in the Bible too you know. There's a message about marriage. There's a message about grace. There's a message about healing. There are all kinds of messages, but satan comes specifically after one message. He doesn't want one seed to take root in the hearts of the believers, **and that my friends is the "Message of the Kingdom."**

** Next take pause, grab your Bible, and read Matthew 13:1-28 and then come back so we can continue. **

In this chapter I am going to tell you in simple terms what is the Message of the Kingdom, so that you can understand it and be able to teach others easily as well because you UNDERSTAND it. That is the key here, understanding. Ask the Father to give you understanding today of the Kingdom Message. Without understanding there is no root to the seed, however with understanding this Message takes root and becomes the largest tree of all garden trees in your heart!

After reading and understanding this, you will be able to easily teach this message. Today is a big day for you if you have made it this far. I am full of joy for you, and so thankful to God that you are reading this. I bless you in the name of the Lord Jesus!

So, listen, satan comes to those who don't understand the Kingdom Message to pull out the seed that was sown. Let's not let him do that anymore. What I'm saying is make sure to understand, stop worrying about life, breathe, relax, and really work right now to focus and understand. This is the message the devil is worried about; this is why he is trying to contain and keep countries locked down. Therefore he has worked overdrive to keep Church doors shut.

Now we see that people are actually going straight to these tyrants to demand them be removed. This is because before the removal first comes the exposure. The enemy cannot help but expose himself, because of the message, this message is now out. This message means the end of his Kingdom, his confidence, and his followers' arrogance! It is the end times for satan and his followers, they are becoming extinct by the zeal of the Lord.

"The Kingdom Message means the destruction of satan and his Kingdom. It means the end of him on our earth forever."

Now, let's go. This is about to get extremely exciting!!

> Matthew 13:31-32 Here is another illustration Jesus used: "The Kingdom of Heaven is like a mustard seed planted in a field. It is the smallest of all seeds, but it becomes the largest of garden plants; it grows into a tree, **and birds come and make nests in its branches."** (One day you will have to hear my preaching on this more in depth)

I've seen this so many times where I've taught this message, I've been teaching it for 10 years, and people hear it. But then a year later they're consumed with it. When it comes to the Kingdom Message, when you hear it at first it may not seem so significant, but later, as you water it and understand and meditate on it more, it becomes the largest tree or largest belief in your heart. If our heart is a garden, it becomes the largest plant in there, and one of the most important things to us.

And what is the Kingdom Message?!

That the Kingdom of God is now activated in us. Through us being made the righteousness of God by faith in Jesus. And we are taking possession of this earth in Jesus' name. We are the heirs of this earth. We are taking dominion from the evil one. We are reconciling all of God's created ordered system back to Him and manifesting the Garden of Eden all over the planet! We are rebuilding, renewing, and restoring broken cities. We are Kings born from Heaven that are taking possession of all the positions of supreme power in the lands, all the gates, all the cities. We are reconciled to reconcile planet earth back to God, and we are blessed with the blessing of Abraham to be a blessing to all nations! All nations shall be blessed! That's the Kingdom Message. You can write that down, declare it, share it, put it up on your wall, whatever you have to do to remember.

Next,

> Matthew 13:33 Jesus also used this illustration: "The Kingdom of Heaven is like the yeast a woman used in making bread. Even though she put only a little yeast in three measures of flour, **it permeated every part of the dough."**

Get it?? The Kingdom is working all the way through, permeating all the earth!!! Why did Jesus say this parable? Well I believe because it was already similarly stated in the book of Daniel. Let's go there real fast.

> Daniel 2:44-45 And in the days of those kings the God of heaven will set up a kingdom that shall never be destroyed, nor shall the kingdom be left to another people. **It shall break in pieces all these kingdoms and bring them to an end, and it shall stand forever,** just as you saw that a stone was cut from a mountain by no human hand, and that it broke in pieces the iron, the bronze, the clay, the silver, and the gold. A great God has made known to the king what shall be after this. The dream is certain, and its interpretation sure."

And then if you read a bit earlier in Daniel chapter 2, you find out that this rock that was cut out, grew into a mountain that filled the whole earth. It is the same concept of the woman with the yeast. Are you seeing it?? The Kingdom Message is a takeover message. We are taking by force what is being given to us because it's our time as Kings of God!

Daniel 2:35 Then the iron, the clay, the bronze, the silver, and the gold, all together were broken in pieces, and became like the chaff of the summer threshing floors; and the wind carried them away, so that not a trace of them could be found. **But the stone that struck the image became a great mountain <u>and filled the whole earth.</u>**

See the Kingdom grows and fills the entire earth. That's what it's like, a small amount of yeast put into dough. **He's telling us in all these different ways the Message of the Kingdom, what the Kingdom is like. Well, it is a takeover plan guys, God is using us to take back control of this earth as his Kings and Priests! Is that really such a far-fetched idea??**

Jesus explained a takeover of the Kingdom of God on earth to the people in parables. But they didn't understand.

Now read,

Luke 19:11 The crowd was listening to everything Jesus said. And because he was nearing Jerusalem, **he told them a story to correct the impression that the Kingdom of God would begin right away.**

See the people didn't understand even after all He had said, how the Kingdom was to manifest.. However, He told them this story to make it clear to them and to "correct the impression that the Kingdom of God would begin right away."

Luke 19:11-17 As they heard these things, He proceeded to tell a parable, because He was near to Jerusalem, and because they supposed that the kingdom of God was to appear immediately.

He said therefore, "A nobleman went into a far country to receive for himself a kingdom and then return. Calling ten of his servants, he gave them ten minas, and said to them, 'Engage in business until I come.' But his citizens hated him and sent a delegation after him, saying, 'We do not want this man to reign over us.' When he returned, having received the kingdom, he ordered these servants to whom he had given the money to be called to him, that he might know what they had gained by doing business. The first came before him, saying, 'Lord, your mina has made ten minas more.' And he said to him, **'Well done, good servant! Because you have been faithful in a very little, you shall have authority over ten cities.'**

Jesus said, The Kingdom is like this, (my paraphrase) some stewards were entrusted with measures of money. Some took that money and put it to work and caused it to multiply for the Master, (Most people today don't want to correlate this chapter Luke 19 with money because they haven't had good experience with money in the past, I think this is an error.) In the Kingdom we learn to think multiplication over addition.

When he returned, he said, "Well done, my good servant," "take charge of ten cities," have government of 10 cities in the Spanish Translation. These people are the Kings of God, the Kingdom Officials, this is a Government of God, the Kingdom of God manifests a Royal Righteous Government, via the Kings of God.

So then when is all this going to happen, what are we doing right now with the age or generation we have been given??! This is a great question we need to be asking ourselves. I don't just want to wander through life acting like I know what's going on, and I hope you don't either. We must really want to know what is going on and what we are to do. We must discover how we are to unite as these born again Kings of God from Heaven to manifest the Will of Jehovah!!!

Because, what's happening in the world right now, is large amounts of believers are realizing that we're not waiting on Jesus to return. We're realizing these thrones and powers that are in the earth are for the Saints of God, and the governing of nations is for the qualified churches **who know the plan of God.** The body of Christ is a governmental body, by the way. Heavens Government is now here.

Alright, let's go to Deuteronomy 28. The Word says this in other places as well. But Deuteronomy 28 is a good place to start.

> Deuteronomy 28:1 "And it shall come to pass, if thou shalt hearken diligently unto the voice of Jehovah thy God, **to take heed to do all His commandments which I command thee this day, that Jehovah thy God <u>will set thee supreme above all nations of the earth</u>**"

This has been the plan throughout the Bible, that one day God's people would listen to Him and obey

Him, then they would become a Holy Nation high above all the nations of the earth.

The UN (United Nations) is a copycat of what the Kingdom Nation is supposed to be. The devil knows who we are in eternity and to a degree how the Kingdom Government will form, he fell from Heaven remember? So, he takes it and tries to corrupt it so we won't use it. We are a Holy Nation high above the nations of this earth. We who believe in Jesus are born from Heaven; we are not born of the earth. We are born again as Children of God, and I am here to teach you that we are also born again as Kings and Priests that are to reign over the earth.

We are the ones qualified and backed by Jehovah the creator of Heaven and earth to lead, and it's time we start stepping it up and stop playing games. We need to rethink our approach at how we steward the earth with God. **We need to start thinking more clearly for our children's and their children's future. A righteous man leaves an inheritance for his children's children says the Word of God. You need to be thinking about that from your heart and trust me when you do God begins to bless you.**

Now there comes a time in this timeline, where the help of God really comes into play. But we're not waiting on the help of God. He has already empowered us and given us more than we need for life. We have to continue to move in faith, <u>but there is a time.</u> And before we go any further, I have to say this.

The imagination in your heart is so important, what you see inside. One time I asked a group of people, maybe 10, "how many of you have ever imagined the people of God, as a nation high above the nations of this world?" None of them had ever done so. **If only people knew the power of imagining the correct story in their hearts. It changes everything.**

I need you to intentionally put into your imagination, the people of God as a nation high above the nations of the earth! Work to begin seeing us as believing ones in Jesus Christ, as the rising Kings that are ruling and reigning, taking back everything from the enemy and manifesting righteousness and blessing throughout every nation!!

Then you really need to press into your imagination (pull the rapture, doom and gloom, and end of planet weeds out), **and then take it to the next level, where you consciously take time to imagine AND speak out, that there is no more evil on the planet.** Can you guys do that? Start by saying "I use my imagination to clearly see God's plan in my heart. I remove any wrong beliefs from my heart now, in Jesus' name."

Imagine a planet with no more evil? David did it. David prophesied it. David said it and so did God!!! A planet with no more evil, remember? The reason the Son of God manifested was to destroy the works of the devil!

> Psalm 37:1-13 Fret not yourself because of evildoers; be not envious of wrongdoers! For they will soon fade like the grass and wither like the green herb. Trust in the Lord, and do good; dwell in the land and befriend faithfulness. Delight yourself in the Lord, and He will give you the desires of your heart. Commit your way to the Lord; trust in Him, and He will act. He will bring forth your righteousness as the light, and your justice as the noonday. Be still before the Lord and wait patiently for Him; fret not yourself over the one who prospers in his way, over the man who carries out evil devices! Refrain from anger, and forsake wrath! Fret not yourself; it tends only to evil.
>
> **For the evildoers shall be cut off, but those who wait for the Lord shall inherit the land.**

In just a little while, the wicked will be no more (non-existent); though you look carefully at his place, he will not be there. But the meek shall inherit the land and delight themselves in abundant peace. The wicked plots against the righteous and gnashes his teeth at him, **but the Lord laughs at the wicked, for he sees <u>that his day is coming.</u>**

Their day is coming. Their day…. A day for the wicked! Remember that as you read. Yes we do our part, but there is a day coming where God steps in.

So, David had this in his imagination and thus he spoke accordingly. He had a vision of the planet without evil on it. You see that? We must have this internal vision too. When we preach, we must be able to paint this picture into the minds of the believer while getting them to erase the false picture that many have from the world, or from false theologies.

Hebrews 8:10-12 **For this is the covenant that I will make with the house of Israel after those days, declares the Lord: I will put my laws into their minds, and write them on their hearts, and I will be their God, and they shall be my people. And they shall not teach, each one his neighbor and each one his brother, saying, 'Know the Lord, <u>for they shall</u>**

all know Me, from the least of them to the greatest. For I will be merciful toward their iniquities, and I will remember their sins no more."

A world where "...they shall all know me" get it? Are you seeing the future that God desires!? And remember His words will accomplish the purpose for which He sent them. No more evil on the earth, only God's people!

Declare it with me: "No more evil on earth, only God's people!"

One day I was listening to this broadcast, and they were talking about the arrests of these different politicians who had committed some serious crimes. One of the broadcasters said, "I just can't imagine that ever happening." And I said, "Oh, that's the problem, you must work on your imagination."

See, whatever you can't really imagine happening you can't really expect to partake in or have. This is how faith works, it works with our imagination which works with our belief. God calls those things that be not as though they were, why? Because He sees them with the eyes of faith, we must practice seeing with the eyes of our heart, our imagination, our faith!

We need to imagine Heaven invading this earth, we need to imagine a day where there will be no more evil on this planet. Imagine if the whole of the Body of Christ embraced and carried this vision, speaking this and declaring "there is no more evil on this planet, there shall be no more wickedness in charge of any place at any time ever on our planet! God's Kings are the Kings of the Earth, under the King of Kings!!" And faith calls things into existence.

And think about it, I mean, just by what we've seen with our faith filled words on healing the sick or speaking over finance, think of the results we have been able to obtain already (I am speaking to those who practice the power of faith filled words). Imagine corporately speaking and believing for the complete removal of all devils from the face of this earth. All evil is gone. A day is coming like that. It may sound strange to some but check this out. Jesus said to pray like this, "Thy kingdom come, Thy will be done on earth, as it is in Heaven."

1 Corinthians 15:25-26 For He must reign **until He has put all His enemies under his feet. The last enemy to be destroyed is death.**

Let me ask you something, are there evil rulers in Heaven??? By now you should be able to say, "Heck no!!" And, if all of Heaven is invading this earth, wouldn't that mean things are to be getting better and better, not worse and worse?? So what are you imagining for in your future? Do you see things getting better and better, or worse and worse? We need to ask people this, because many are unconsciously unaware of what their subconscious is believing for.

In Ephesians it talks about the Church as the group that is to make known the manifold wisdom of God to the authorities and "rulers" in the high places. We are actually supposed to make known to the rulers of this world, that if they don't worship and obey Jehovah and his Son, they are no longer rulers. That is the reality that we must not fear to announce. Imagine the Church having meetings and coming up with strategies on how to make known the manifold wisdom of God to the leaders in their cities!! The Bible says we should be doing this.

> Ephesians 3:10-11 God's purpose in all this was to use the church to display His wisdom in its rich variety to all the unseen rulers and authorities in the heavenly places. This was His eternal plan, which He carried out through Christ Jesus our Lord.

Ephesians 1:9-10 **God has now revealed to us His mysterious will** regarding Christ—which is to fulfill His own good plan. And this is the plan: At the right time **He will bring everything together under the authority of Christ—everything in heaven and on earth.**

Isn't this powerful, <u>the mystery of God's will has been revealed!</u> We should all know His will!!! If anyone doesn't know God's will read and study Ephesians 1:9-10 with them.

People sometimes say "Cory we can't know God's will, His ways are too high." I say "well now we can, and we have the mind of Christ. Plus, the mystery of His will HAS BEEN MADE KNOWN TO US in Ephesians 1:9-10!! To bring all things in Heaven and on earth under the authority of Christ!"

This Kingdom, this Dominion of God has been activated in the earth. Man always had it but righteousness was needed to operate with it. Now we have become the righteousness of God through Christ Jesus!! This Kingdom and its Government is going to grow and grow and crush every other Kingdom.

But what has happened? Somehow the Church's doctrines, and history of the fathers of faith over the past 2000 years has mostly been hijacked and twisted.

This has caused many believers to use their faith for the wrong things, and in the wrong direction. They've been thinking they are in the first century and believing for another anti-Christ to come, another tribulation, another bunch of famines, and everything bad around the corner. They're using their faith, they're speaking it. Do we believe words have power to make impact? Yes!

Well, we can't have the Church speaking and teaching we're in the last days of our planet. But rather it's the last days of satan and his rule on earth, and we shall rebuild, renew, and restore the broken places. God is reconciling the world back to Himself! This is a huge difference.

God says "Sit at my right hand until I make all your enemies your footstool" "the last enemy to be defeated is death." God is in us, and we are bringing down these people with these evil spirits and their whole Kingdom. We are bringing them down and we must stop being soft. **This is a military operation from Heaven.** This is a military operation and wait till you hear what we are about to read. What we are about to read might only be understood by the Davids and the Calebs at heart, because most of the world is coming out of some politically correct spell. That is exactly what it is "a spell." Break free and stop being politically correct in Jesus name! Who cares what other people think, I care what God thinks.

God's not going to do all this glorious work. He lives in us, he needs us to move as the Body. He needs the Church to do what the Church is supposed to do. We must believe that God is willing to move on our behalf while we take steps towards a brighter future bringing an end to this corruption. Let's go to Romans 8.

> Romans 8:18-21 For I consider that the sufferings of this present time are not worth comparing with the glory that is to be revealed to us. **For the creation waits with eager longing for the revealing of the sons of God.** For the creation was subjected to futility, not willingly, but because of him who subjected it, **in hope that the creation itself will be set free from its bondage to corruption and obtain the freedom of the glory of the children of God.**

This says the creation is waiting for the Sons of God (plural). Very important for the Churches and

Leaders to know this right here. This one line you can use with the pastors and it opens up their mind.

I usually say, "You are telling us we're waiting on the Son of God to come in the clouds, but this says the creation is waiting on the Sons of God (plural) to manifest and set it free. Which one is it pastor?" Then watch as they reel for answers. I am about tired of seeing pastors make up answers to questions they don't know. If you don't know the answer say "I don't know" and God will bless you, and probably give you the answer and much more because you humbled yourself.

Waiting on Jesus to return to make things better is not the Sons of God manifesting and setting creation free! One is waiting on the Son, the other is the Sons taking action. These are two opposing approaches. Now it is time, we will solve this issue.

Alright family, I'm gonna take you on an adventure in this Word and I will show you we are rooting out the evil ones. Hallelujah! I don't know exactly how this will play out in each nation, but if you don't know God, and you're trying to rule a nation, be gone and step down! Or get crushed by the Kingdom of God in the name above all names Jesus!

You can't try to lead people in God's creation, especially GOD'S PEOPLE with His power and His life living inside of them. You can't do that in His creation, nor any other planet in this Universe if you don't serve the King of kings.

The works of satan are being extinguished and brought to nothing. These tyrants are being exposed for who they are and brought to nothing, free-masons, witches, luciferians, satanists, all of them are being pushed out into the open by the flood of God's light and removed as the impurities and blemishes they are.

People say Cory you are harsh. I would say no no no, you have become soft and numb to what is really going on and what the solutions really are. Which we will see shortly, and you probably won't call me harsh anymore after you hear what God says about this through the prophet Isaiah.

We are now going to read Isaiah 14.

Isaiah 14:1-2 For Jehovah will have mercy on Jacob, and will yet choose Israel, **and set them in rest in their own land; and the stranger shall be united to them, and they shall be joined to the house of Jacob. And the peoples shall take them and bring them to their place;** and the house of Israel shall possess them in the land of Jehovah for servants and handmaids; **and they shall take them captive whose captives they were, and they shall rule over their oppressors.**

Pause.

Oh my goodness, you know, in Daniel seven, it says the kingdoms of this world will be handed over to the Saints. Let's talk about that for a minute. Kingdoms Handed over? They will take them to their own place? Israel will possess the nations? They will make captives of their captors and rule over their oppressors?

Are you guys seeing anything!?

"Hey, King Cory, King Paul, King Lindsay, you see what's happening in our nation!!!?" "Help us! We know other people can't stand against this pressure, against these attacks. Will you stand here with us, in this position of power in our nation, and bless our nation with the blessing that God has placed on you!?" "Come with us. Come, we hand you the nation!"

Do you get it?? All nations shall be blessed is the gospel. Eventually the nations will catch on and realize that the only ones able to lead are **God's**

Chosen, those who have passed His tests and qualifications, and **those who worship and obey Him!**

No one else on planet earth except those who follow Jesus and have been born again have authority over all evil.

"And the house of Israel will possess the nations." Imagine being a Jew reading that back in the day. This is why I said they knew that one day they were going to take over the world. This is why everyone has tried to attack Israel. Because the devil believes the Bible too. However, those of us in Christ have been grafted in. It is not just the country of Israel like many have thought. It's not about Jew or Gentile anymore. It's about Sons and Daughters of God with the blessing, the promise and the faith of Abraham.

It's about letting God's Kings be Kings over the earth. "Let my Kings Be Kings" I hear the Lord say.

"They will make captives of their captors and rule over their oppressors." Many people are probably like, "Well that's not nice thing to do brother." Well then you might want to tear that page out of your Bible if we are just picking and choosing how we interpret God's Word.

And like I've been saying, we've been preached some fluffy stuff guys. Many have grown up in an age of don't step on people's toes. Have you not read the Old Testament and how whole wicked cities and nations were leveled??? Surely you at least remember the story of Sodom and Gomorrah. What else are we to do with the wicked? Leave them alone to form again and rise and build their tyrannical systems, cities, and murder humanity??

Let's keep reading,

Isaiah 14:3-27 For Jehovah will have mercy on Jacob, and will yet choose Israel, and set them in rest in their own land; and the stranger shall be united to them, and they shall be joined to the house of Jacob. And the peoples shall take them and bring them to their place; and the house of Israel shall possess them in the land of Jehovah for servants and handmaids; and they shall take them captive whose captives they were, and they shall rule over their oppressors. And it shall come to pass in the day that Jehovah shall give thee rest from thy sorrow and from thy trouble and from the hard bondage wherein thou wast made to serve, that thou shalt take up this proverb against the king of Babylon, and say, How hath the oppressor ceased,—the exactress of gold ceased.

Jehovah hath broken the staff of the wicked, the sceptre of the rulers. He that smote the peoples in wrath with a relentless stroke, he that ruled the nations in anger, is persecuted unsparingly. The whole earth is at rest, is quiet: they break forth into singing. Even the cypresses rejoice at thee, the cedars of Lebanon, [saying,] Since thou art laid down, no feller is come up against us.

Sheol from beneath is moved for thee to meet [thee] at thy coming, stirring up the dead for thee, all the he-goats of the earth; making to rise from their thrones all the kings of the nations. All of them shall answer and say unto thee, Art thou also become powerless as we; art thou become like unto us!— Thy pomp is brought down to Sheol, the noise of thy lyres: the maggot is spread under thee, and worms cover thee. **How art thou fallen from heaven, Lucifer, son of the morning! Thou art cut down to the ground, that didst prostrate the nations!**

And thou that didst say in thy heart, I will ascend into the heavens, I will exalt my throne above the stars of God, and I will sit upon the mount of assembly, in the recesses of the north; I will ascend above the heights of the clouds, I will be like the Most High: none the less art thou brought down to Sheol, to the recesses of the pit. They that see thee shall narrowly look upon thee; they shall consider thee, [saying,] Is this the man that made the earth to tremble, that shook kingdoms; [that] made the world as a wilderness, and overthrew the cities thereof; [that] dismissed not his prisoners homewards? —All the kings of the nations, all of them, lie in glory, every one in his own house; but thou art cast out of thy grave like an abominable branch, covered with the slain—those thrust through with the sword, that go down to the stones of the pit: like a carcass trodden under foot. Thou shalt not be joined with them in burial; for thou hast destroyed thy land, hast slain thy people. <u>Of the seed of evildoers no mention shall be made for ever.</u>

Prepare ye slaughter for his children, because of the iniquity of their fathers; that they may not rise up and possess the earth, nor fill the face of the world with cities. For I will rise up against them, saith Jehovah of hosts, and cut off from Babylon name and remnant, and scion and descendant, saith Jehovah. And I will make it a possession for the bittern, and pools of water; and I will sweep it with the besom of destruction, saith Jehovah of hosts. Jehovah of hosts hath sworn saying, Assuredly as I have thought, so shall it come to pass; and as I have purposed, it shall stand: to break the Assyrian in my land;

and upon my mountains will I tread him under foot; and his yoke shall depart from off them, and his burden depart from off their shoulders.

This is the counsel which is purposed concerning the whole earth; and this is the hand which is stretched out upon all the nations. For Jehovah of hosts hath purposed, and who shall frustrate [it]? And his hand is stretched out, and who shall turn it back?

Well, that's what's going on guys. That's the plan of God for global freedom from evil, the complete removal of evil off the face of the earth prophesied by the Lord Himself! That's what's happening guys. On the day the Lord gives you relief from suffering and turmoil and cruel bondage, you will take up this taunt!! You will read aloud Isaiah 14:1-27!!

And I tell people, "Man! Things are gonna get better and better. God's people are rising up whether you believe it or not!" It's happening. But believing it, sharing and declaring it, really helps us to manifest it quicker.

Understanding this Kingdom Message, and that evil is not to remain on our planet is going to help you personally succeed in life. You're no longer going to be waiting for something bad to happen in a state of fear. You're going to be looking for something good to happen, believing for good in the earth, and you're going to receive good!

As things get better you're going to come up with business ideas. You'll probably want to have more kids, get lands, plant food, and all these amazing things that most Christians say why bother, it's the last days. Instead you will produce real fruit, fruit that remains, Kingdom fruit!

This is good news for us who give our hearts and lives to the Will of the Father, not so good news for those who choose to follow an evil, defeated, judged spirit. Their time is running short. We can and should pray for them to repent and be loosed from satan's deception.

Alright, let's go to the book of Acts.

> Acts 1:1-3 In the first book, O Theophilus, I have dealt with all that Jesus began to do and teach, until the day when he was taken up, after he had given commands through the Holy Spirit to the apostles whom he had chosen. He presented himself alive to them after his suffering by many proofs, appearing to them during forty days and speaking about the kingdom of God.

Imagine hearing Jesus speak for 40 days about the Kingdom. How glorious that will be. What it will look like when God's Kings have taken over.

Acts 1:4-6 And while staying with them he ordered them not to depart from Jerusalem, but to wait for the promise of the Father, which, He said, "You heard from Me; for John baptized with water, but you will be baptized with the Holy Spirit not many days from now." **So when they had come together, they asked Him, "Lord, will you at this time restore the kingdom to Israel?"**

Interesting question, right? Because that was on their mind. The Savior would come and then they would have dominion over the earth, that was what they had concluded from the Prophets. But again, they were off in their interpretation just a bit.

What does Jesus say next?

Acts 1:7-8 He said to them, "It is not for you to know times or seasons that the Father has fixed by His own authority. But you will receive power when the Holy Spirit has come upon you, and you will be My witnesses in Jerusalem and in all Judea and Samaria, and to the end of the earth."

Now, again, it's talking about a time and a date set by the Father when the people of God will take over. I will say this again, there is a day, a day when the people of God take over the world. I don't know how people have missed this. A time and a date to restore the Kingdom or Dominion to Israel (those in Christ, the seed of Abraham).

They were asking partly because what we just read in Isaiah 14, it said that Israel would be given all the nations and they would take them to their places so that they would be the rulers. But see they didn't realize how Kingdom manifested, which is probably why he needed 40 days with them to talk about things concerning the Kingdom.

We are this mountain in the Lord that keeps on rising and rising, and satan keeps on shrinking and shrinking until he becomes irrelevant and forgotten. His systems become irrelevant, because of the glorious systems we are bringing forward. And I wish it was all here manifested already, right now. That would be awesome.

However, we have work to do, and all of the generations before us are watching and hoping that we figure this out. The generations that missed it, they got deceived and complacent. They bought into lies and therefore, many did not take steps of faith to make the world better for the generations to come; not taking steps of faith to get educated, not crushing and exposing this evil.

Let us not waste our generation and hand it off worse for our children. Now is the time!!!

So, what are we going to do with this time God has put us in?? Are we gonna sit around now that we have this revelation, this Message of the Kingdom Takeover??! No!

We're gonna take it by force, and it's also going to be handed over to us. It's twofold. However, both can happen simultaneously. I was thinking about this with God. I said "How do we take it by force, and it be given??" I hear the Lord say "If someone were to reach out to hand you a pencil could you take it by force??" I said yup, got it Father. I believe we will take Dominion over the Nations by force, while it's being handed over, because it is long overdue! Give me that!!!

This earth is ours, the meek inherit the earth!

The creation is groaning and waiting on us to wake up and take over! But let me say this, we are Kings, and the Kings of God emerging over nations are to be an example of the Father. Meaning these Kings emerging will be like powerful Heavenly Father figures, full of wisdom, love, and power to bless their nation, as well as other nations! The moral sound minded people will want to follow them. Those who reject God will become non-existent.

Psalm 140:11 Let not the man of [evil] tongue be established in the earth: evil shall hunt the man of violence to [his] ruin.

CH.6 JESUS HAS ALL AUTHORITY IN HEAVEN AND EARTH

Let's start with a prayer:

"Father God, we just thank you that we are gathered together today, in the name of your son Jesus. Lord, we know that all authority and power has been given to you in Heaven and on earth. I ask that you help Holy Spirit to make this real to us. That greater are you who is in us, than he who is in the world. I pray for the removal of all fear! Let truth, and love be released to uproot all fear. "And you will know the truth, the truth will make us free in the name of Jesus, amen."

Okay, so I'm going to start with a quick story. I received Jesus in a prison cell about ten years ago. I was possessed by many devils; I heard them and saw them for four years. I was in and out of the mental hospital, and in and out of the jail.

You know, when you tell people you're hearing voices in your head that want to kill you, they kinda freak out. And they're like, "You're crazy. Oh, my gosh, you're gonna kill somebody," and they typically call the police on you. So, I was in and out of jail over and over, but I heard these voices and I didn't know what they were. I thought it was just the government, you know, using some technologies to try to get me to shoot somebody. You know, like all these people you see on TV that do crazy shootings. They usually say the same thing, "I was hearing voices in my head that threatened me to do it."

Well, there actually is technology that allows people to put voices as frequencies into people's inner ear, but it's dark, and they work with the devil. These demons obviously speak as they did in the Bible.

Matthew 8:29 And behold, they cried out, saying, What have we to do with thee, Son of God? **hast Thou come here before the time to torment us?**

I wonder when their appointed time is, could it be now??! Let me ask you this, how could it not be now? Jesus is resurrected and ascended to the right hand of the Father as King over the Nations!

Finally, I ended up with a weapons charge, because I thought I found the root of this mind control stuff, the man behind it all. But in reality, these voices had set up a plan to make me think it was him, the guy probably had no idea what was going on. Anyways I thought I found the guy behind this torturous plan and pulled out an SKS rifle on him. Thanks to God that he grabbed the gun and tried to discharge the clip.

This was in the middle of town. Thankfully I didn't hurt anybody, so I grabbed my gun and ran. There was no way I was going to get out of this. Many people saw what had happened. And so you know, when you hear voices in your head that say constantly for four years, "I'm going to kill you when you go to sleep" and all kinds of vulgar statements, all day, and all night you carry some weapons.

That's how the devil tried to take me out. Before that happened, he tried to get me to bow down to him with two of my friends. I was freaked out and said no. But the thing is, I didn't even really know what or who the devil was, what satan was and I didn't know really anything about Jesus either.

So, when these "friends" said, bow down to this spirit, be like us, I was like "um no," why would I need to do that, plus the room felt super creepy. But a bunch of my friends worshiped the devil, and I didn't realize what that was all about until after many years. They were playing these mind games on me and others, crazy stuff that they do on the dark side. One of these friends was murdered, the other one is paralyzed from the neck down filled with demons. I tried to go and cast them out but was unsuccessful. It seemed successful but they later came back. Things will always end bad for those who follow a defeated, judged spirit.

So anyways, I'm in prison, doing a year and a half for this charge. I remember sitting there one day thinking, I don't want to get out of here and live that life anymore. So, I decided to pray. I said "God, I don't want to hurt people anymore, would you forgive me for the way I've been living? Would you teach me your ways?" After I prayed that I had the first tear drop I could remember in years. I looked up and just went about my day, nothing had changed. I didn't really feel any different. There's a bigger backstory: I'm just going to tell you the brief point of how I know Jesus is King and His power is supreme.

About four days later, there was this guy in the prison who went by the name "Country" that I had been following around for months, because he said he had to tell me something and he can only tell me at the right time. I'm like TELL ME NOW and he wouldn't. Anyways, I made friends with this guy. I walked up to his cell one day and he said, "Cory, don't you know all the answers that you're seeking are in the Bible?"

He said, "All the answers you're seeking are in the Bible." And I said, "No, they're not. No, they're not." And the reason I said that is because I remembered trying to find the answers in the Bible when I was all messed up hearing voices. I was reading the book of Ezekiel, about flying chariots and all these heads and different kinds of creatures and things. I was trying to find answers for my life, and I couldn't figure out how to apply that book. And I read the whole book of Ezekiel, by the way, because that's where I started. I didn't have anyone tell me that you probably shouldn't start with the book of Ezekiel.

Anyways, I got back into my cell for the evening, and I had a Bible. And it's kind of looking at me. So, I said, "Okay, I'm gonna read this again." I grabbed it and this time it opened to Ephesians chapter two, a much better place to start reading!! You know where the Bible reads, "...*you have been following the prince of the powers of the air, the spirit who works in those who are disobedient, ...but now you have been saved by grace through faith, and this is not of your own doing, it is a gift from God.*"

I read that chapter, and as I was reading, I realized that the Bible was speaking this word to me. These words were glowing with this white light, and it was going into my eyes, like holograms. It literally looked and felt like words were going into me, I saw it happening.

In that moment all these demonic voices, and there were probably about 40 voices I heard, in a moment, a second, every single one of them stopped talking. Complete silence in my mind for the first time in four years, and I could no longer see them either. Everything shut off in a moment. I remember feeling hope for the first time.

I said, "Wow, maybe I will live, maybe there is a purpose for my life." Before, I couldn't understand the Bible, but now all of a sudden I am understanding it, and it felt like it was speaking directly to me!

I'm like, "Holy cow, what the heck is going on?" I just kept reading nonstop every day for the rest of my time in prison. I thought, God gave me this time to learn this book. I said, I'm gonna read it and read it and read it. I took all day long from around five in the morning till around midnight, every single day reading my Bible.

I would go out and work out and walk laps in the day, but I made it a point to understand it. I said, I have to know what this Word is saying. I don't want to be tricked anymore. I had been tricked my whole life. I was skeptical also of the pastors that were coming in the prisons, I didn't trust them either.

I said, "You're going to teach me God, if you can teach others your word, you can teach me too." So, I developed a friendship with the Holy Spirit. I realized He was my teacher, and He would answer me, and I could hear Him very well. When you have nothing else going on around you and you're sitting in a prison cell, it's pretty easy to hear Holy Spirit when you honor Him, respect Him, and approach Him like a teacher.

I'm saying all this because I developed a pretty unique perspective on the Bible. While I was in there, I saw in the Word that God's people were supposed to be taking over the world! I saw that the devil was judged, and I knew it to be true from my experience with Jesus cleaning house in a moment! I saw that all you had to do is believe in Jesus and give your life to Him. The devil was gone from me, and I had been translated out of darkness into light. All things were made new for me, and I knew it.

Then I saw that we were purchased by the blood of Jesus to be Kings that reign on the earth. I realized that I was a son of God, potentially a king, and we're supposed to be leaders of the earth. So, I got out of prison, very excited to meet other Christians like this.

I was like, "Yes, I am going to meet some Kings! Where have I been!!?" "And we're going to take over and we're going to crush this devil. We are gonna finish him off." And yeah, I was kind of shocked when I got out of prison. I started going to different churches, all kinds of churches actually. If their lights were on, I went in.

And the thing that I want to point out in this chapter is, I quickly noticed that the majority of the people in the Church were afraid of the devil.

They thought he wasn't judged yet. Maybe the reason why is they never really experienced a full blast demonic attack and then deliverance. Then also at the same time, they didn't understand from the scriptures that satan has been judged. I noticed people were waiting for all kinds of things before they could have complete victory. The "occupy mentality." We are not in a waiting room. We are taking over the earth! It is our inheritance; it is ours in Christ!

I'm going to bring the Complete Victory teaching out now! Complete Victory Now is what Jesus paid for! Man, it's very powerful when you understand what I'm about to share with you guys. What I learned in that prison cell. That I had complete victory in this earth over all evil now and forever. This chapter here is a definite piece to the Kingdom Message.

Now I had to make sure of this and study a bit more.. But that was my main question, when I read the Bible, is it complete victory? Is it 100% victory or is there a (but). What I discovered and 10 years later can still prove, is that we have complete victory now!!! I proved it to myself. And I probably wouldn't follow this gospel if it wasn't 100% victory. I would probably just do my life. But I know that 100% victory is in Christ Jesus, it's the only way. He is the supreme King and carries the supreme spiritual power in the earth. Jehovah is a good Father, and Jesus is a good Lord. And so, I yielded my complete self to do the will of the Father.

Time went on, and I got invited to preach at this church. I've told this story before, but I'll tell it one more time. I ended up getting invited by the pastor to preach, and it was a church of around 100-200 people. I just started preaching that the devil is already judged from John 16:11. So when the Holy Spirit comes, He's gonna convict the world to be in the wrong about three areas, righteousness, sin, judgment, because the prince of this world has been judged!!!

Holy Spirit wanted me to teach that part. I started teaching and I asked "Why are you worrying about him? Why are you afraid of the devil?" I said, "Why? Why are you sick and in poverty and suffering, and speaking it all out?"

I was like, "You're supposed to speak victory, you're supposed to command the devil out of your life, and live free!!" I preached like that for about 10 minutes. Then I said, "Everyone, close your eyes." I prayed in the name of Jesus saying, "I command all you devils out of this church, out of these people, and out of this city in the name of Jesus." The word went forth like a shock-wave.

And what I am about to share is very important. After the church service there were three men that approached me, the Pastor included. They said, "Cory you can't talk about the devil that way or he will come after you." They tried to scare me about the devil, but it didn't work. Because I was like, "What do you mean he's gonna come after me? Me? I'm coming after him. Don't you know he is judged and we have complete power and victory over him?!!" "You all have it wrong" I said.

Now I don't fill my mind all day with thinking about how I can come after the devil. But I do think about how we can implement strategies superior from

Heaven to break the hold of darkness off the nations. How can we innovate, create, and release light that crushes and exposes the nature of satan, removing his residue off our earth? How can we do that? And I realized these three leaders were carrying fear of a defeated, judged, under our feet enemy.

These leaders were subconsciously imparting to their followers that we didn't have complete victory yet, and that we should fear him. I can only imagine what type of anxiety and fruit that belief would carry. And they were the elders of the church! No wonder the congregation was in a perilous condition complaining for an hour about all their problems for "prayer time." It looked like total defeat compared to what I was reading and experiencing.

I said, "You guys, he's been judged. He's been defeated." But see, in the Church, lots of believers don't really get this truth because they weren't possessed by devils, so I kinda get it. Also, those three men became my good friends. I was able to teach them a lot, but they also taught me a lot about life, and I am eternally grateful.

Next, we're going to do some scriptures!! And thanks for hearing a bit of my testimony.

1 John 3:8-10 Whoever makes a practice of sinning is of the devil, for the devil has been sinning from the beginning. **The reason the Son of God appeared was to destroy the works of the devil.** No one born of God makes a practice of sinning, for God's seed abides in him; and he cannot keep on sinning, because he has been born of God. By this it is evident who are the children of God, and who are the children of the devil: whoever does not practice righteousness is not of God, nor is the one who does not love his brother.

The reason the Son of God appeared **was to destroy the works of the devil.**

Let's also look at **"No one born of God** makes a practice of sinning, for God's seed abides in him; and he cannot keep on sinning, because he has been born of God. **By this it is evident who are the children of God, and who are the children of the devil:** whoever does not practice righteousness is not of God, nor is the one who does not love his brother."

See, there's a lot of people out there that will try to tell you there's no such thing as a devil. The devil just means your ego, that there's no spirit of the devil, it's just your flesh or carnal thinking. And when you do that, you cause a lot of issues in your ability to walk victorious. Because you're fooling yourself, there is a devil, but we have victory over him.

Also there are many groups that claim everyone is born again already, or born again is just an internal awakening. This is also a problem because it is not true and these sects confuse many people with their fine sounding doctrines. Born from God in the Greek means born from above! satan is a spirit that works in those who are disobedient. The reason the Son of God manifested was to destroy the works of the devil. Some groups think if they just don't talk about satan he will disappear. They think it is easier than enforcing his Judgment. Watch out for these people.

> John 1:11-13   He came to his own, and His own received Him not; **but as many as received Him, to them gave He [the] right to be children of God,** to those that believe on His name; **who have been born, not of blood, nor of flesh's will, nor of man's will, <u>but of God.</u>**

Now the reason Jesus came was to destroy the works of the devil. That's the reason; destroy the works of the devil. We are His Body, and we are finishing that work. Yes, the work is finished in the spirit and he has been judged in the spirit.

Now it's time we enforce it and kick all evil off our planet into the lake of fire, their place of torment in the name of Jesus!

> John 12:31 "Now is [the] judgment of this world; **now shall the prince of this world be cast out"**

Now satan will be cast out. Say with me "satan we cast you out of our earth in the name of Jesus!!"

Daniel 7:26 and 27 mentions that his power will be extinguished or consumed until the end when translated from Hebrew. You know, I was looking at something in Spanish the other day that was hanging on the wall. The word of this fire extinguisher device in Spanish is, "extinctor" and I was thinking, "that is what we are doing, **we are the extinctors of the devil."** We are the extinctors of the devil and his power in this earth, we're removing the residue of him. We are making him extinct.

When people start understanding this Kingdom Message that we have been learning, there are groups of people that will come around and try to deceive. For real, the devil really doesn't want people to get this message because it means the end of him. And they'll try to say all kinds of things to get you caught up in arguments or stuck on details. They try to keep you away from simplicity of the Kingdom Message and your clear forward focus. Just do like Jesus did and keep moving forward towards your goals.

I have even seen groups saying that angels and demons are not real, everyone is already baptized with the Holy Spirit and on and on. When confronted with scriptures they just wiggle around, get nervous, and maybe will give you an opinion. We don't need opinions of man; we need truth and revelation from God's Word. Make sure who you follow is preaching the Word of God, not their opinions. Do they have a Bible with them? Do they know God's plan of Reconciliation??

Don't let people contaminate the simplicity of what is the Kingdom Message. Don't let people take you down rabbit trails and get you stuck. **Keep it simple "All of Heaven is invading this earth."**

The Bible says we are born of God. If you go to the Greek, it says born from Heaven, born from above. I just want to point that out. There's a born again experience. You get born from above, born from

Heaven. You have a new lineage, you have new DNA, you have a new Spirit that is now one with your spirit, and it is the Spirit of the Living God. You become one with His Spirit, and you become a son of God through this rebirth.

> John 1:11-13 He came to His own, and His own received Him not; **but as many as received Him, to them gave He [the] right to be children of God, to those that believe on His name; who have been born, not of blood, nor of flesh's will, nor of man's will, but of God.**

Now, that's kind of a lot to say, but I need to let you all know because it's a big deal. When people start getting this Kingdom Message, the devil comes with a few tricks, and I have seen them over and over throughout the past ten years preaching this.

One of them sounds like this "We're all one brother" or "Everyone is already born again filled with the Holy Ghost they just need to realize it" or "Hell really just means this or that." Lots of nice sounding ideas out there, but not what the Bible says. It is good to also stay out of debates with people who are trying to prove their points over doing the will of God, or you might end up battling egos and devils. Read your Word for yourself, don't rely on man, don't rely on me. You don't need to try and fit in with the coolest groups and seek the approval of man, rather seek the approval of God.

Next, we are going to be in the NLT version.

John 16:5-11 "But now I am going away to the One who sent Me, and not one of you is asking where I am going. Instead, you grieve because of what I've told you. But in fact, it is best for you that I go away, because if I don't, the Advocate won't come. **If I do go away, then I will send Him to you. And when He comes, He will convict the world of its sin, and of God's righteousness, and of the coming judgment.** The world's sin is that it refuses to believe in Me. Righteousness is available because I go to the Father, and you will see me no more. **Judgment will come because the ruler of this world <u>has already been judged.</u>**

You catching revelation here?? Jesus said that when the Holy Spirit comes, He's going to teach the world about three things. About sin, righteousness, and judgment because satan has already been judged. People this is important because many read the book of Revelation where it talks about this falling of the devil, and because it's in the book of Revelation they assume that it's in our future.

Churches have taught that Revelation is only a future book, when it's actually a book to warn the churches of "**what must soon take place**" in regards to the destruction of Jerusalem. Soon means soon, by the way. The devil was already judged. That was a picture of his judgment in the spirit in the book of Revelation. Remember Jesus "saw satan fall like lightning from Heaven!" Saw it, past tense.

We have this issue in the Church where people are waiting on this judgment of the devil. They think when Christ returns, He's gonna judge the devil again. But if we read the words of Jesus, he says that the devil has been judged. "I saw satan fall like lightning!" The disciples had power over the evil spirits in the name of Jesus before the cross, because satan fell before the cross. Jesus said now is the time for the prince of this world to be driven out.

So, what does this all mean? Well, if the devil has been judged, that means there was a court that sat and stripped his power; a court has to sit for a judgment to take place.

And if you read Daniel 7, let's go there real fast...

Daniel 7:26-27 **"But then the court will pass judgment, and all his power will be taken away and completely destroyed.** Then the sovereignty, power, and greatness of all the kingdoms under heaven will be given to the holy people of the Most High. **His kingdom will last forever, and all rulers will serve and obey Him."**

If we realize the devil is judged, then we also need to realize we are in the time of taking possession of "all the Kingdoms under the whole heavens." Hallelujah!

Matthew 28:18 All authority in heaven and on earth has been given to Me.

That's how we can also know the court has sat. You all see that? Because the authority is in Jesus's hands now, **all of it.** He has all of it. That means the devil has no authority, no rights on this earth anymore because he has been judged.

The Holy Spirit when He comes, He was to preach three specific things, one of them being THE DEVIL IS ALREADY JUDGED!!!!!!!! John 16:11

> Colossians 1:15-16 He is the image of the invisible God, the firstborn of all creation. For by Him all things were created, in heaven and on earth, visible and invisible, whether thrones or dominions or rulers or authorities—all things were created through Him and for Him.

These thrones, these are positions of power, and all of them were created by and for the Lord Jesus. Many are starting to learn that these are ordained for the people of God in Christ. There are currently pastors, teachers, and believers who are Bible minded, stepping up. They're saying "No, hold on. These thrones are our positions of power, this is our earth, and now is the time for satan to be driven out!!!!" Believers are starting to get it and starting to **BELIEVE IT!**

Say this with me, "This earth is ours in Jesus name!!"

God's people must lead, not just in the church but in every area of life. The Bible says when the godly are in power, the people rejoice. You know the Bible says that when the wicked are in power, the people go into hiding. That's what has happened to many, but we are coming out with shouts of joy and massive revelation that has the capacity to set all nations free!!

By the way, talking about the devil doesn't make him come around you. It doesn't make him bigger and badder. When we talk about the devil, we're coming from a position of victory. He is actually under our feet! But he needs to be under everyone's feet if you know what I mean. Some people think that "Cory, you're talking about the devil, we shouldn't say his name, right?" Because they think it makes him bigger and badder. "What you focus on you magnify," they say.

Well, we are focusing on his removal off the planet and the establishment of the Kingdom of God, so that is what we will get. He can't get bigger and badder, he is Judged by God. He has been convicted as guilty. Now we just need to let the world hear it preached so they can believe and come out from fear of a defeated spirit. We also need many to step up and help get this message out to the world. The future generations depend on it!

We must address what the actual problem is, not deny it, so that we are able to get the solutions from God. We are not problem minded but rather solution minded! Kingdom minded!

Colossians 2:6-15 **And now, just as you accepted Christ Jesus as your Lord, you must continue to follow Him. Let your roots grow down into Him, and let your lives be built on Him. Then your faith will grow strong in the truth you were taught, and you will overflow with thankfulness.**

Don't let anyone capture you with empty philosophies and high-sounding nonsense that come from human thinking and from the spiritual powers of this world, rather than from Christ. For in Christ lives all the fullness of God in a human body. So you also are complete through your union with Christ, who is the head over every ruler and authority.

When you came to Christ, you were "circumcised," but not by a physical procedure. Christ performed a spiritual circumcision—the cutting away of your sinful nature. For you were buried with Christ when you were baptized. And with Him you were raised to new life because you trusted the mighty power of God, who raised Christ from the dead.

You were dead because of your sins and because your sinful nature was not yet cut away. Then God made you alive with Christ, for He forgave all our sins. He canceled the record of the charges against us and took it away by nailing it to the cross. **In**

this way, He disarmed the spiritual rulers and authorities. He shamed them publicly by his victory over them on the cross.

Powerful!! Next, I want to talk about Ephesians. We're hearing about the power of the rulers and authorities being disarmed, but we must realize we have access to the full armor of God. I want to point something out to you.

Ephesians 6:10-12 Finally, be strong in the Lord and in the strength of His might. **Put on the whole armor of God, that you may be able to stand against the schemes of the devil. For we do not wrestle against flesh and blood, but against the rulers, against the authorities, against the cosmic powers over this present darkness, against the spiritual forces of evil in the heavenly places.**

I share this <u>not</u> because the devil is big and bad. I share this because we need to know where the battle is.

Paul said our battle is against the principalities and powers of wickedness in the high places. That's where the battle is and finally people are waking up to this. It's our battle until they are all removed. The truth is, we need to understand this world is ours, and that God's plan is to restore the planet back to Himself, and to be in all and through all.

And for all of you who think the battle is over, why did Paul feel led to write this letter to the Ephesians after the cross?? It's over when all the thrones and positions of power in this earth are occupied by the "Saints of God," and all nations are blessed. The last enemy to be defeated is death. One day death will even be gone from this planet. Why? You should know this answer by now. All of Heaven's light, glory and eternity is invading this earth, swallowing it up!

There's nothing stopping us from 100% victory; it is the will of the Father. The final battle in my view, is believing and manifesting God's promise for us to "possess the cities of our enemies." That's what the promise was to Abraham, that we would take possession of the cities of our enemies and through us, all nations on earth will be blessed.

We take possession of the cities (gates), and then the blessing of the righteous comes down, that light of God, that Glory of God comes down over all the cities world-wide.

Proverbs 11:10-11 When it goeth well with the righteous, the city rejoiceth; and when the wicked perish, there is shouting. **By the blessing of the upright the city is exalted;** but it is overthrown by the mouth of the wicked.

As more people understand that this is God's plan, we can move into harmony with Heaven's Reign much faster. So please share this writing and support the advancement of these truths. Through our believing hearts we are moving into harmony with Heaven and manifesting it here on earth now!

One more scripture; let's look at what actually happened when Jesus ascended. This is just as important to discuss as the resurrection in my opinion.

Revelation 5:1-10   And I saw on the right hand of him that sat upon the throne a book, written within and on the back, sealed with seven seals. And I saw a strong angel proclaiming with a loud voice, Who [is] worthy to open the book, and to break its seals? And no one was able in the heaven, or upon the earth, or underneath the earth, to open the book, or to regard it.

And *I* wept much because no one had been found worthy to open the book nor to regard it. And one of the elders says to me, Do not weep. Behold, the lion which [is] of the tribe of Judah, the root of David, has overcome [so as] to open the book, and its seven seals.

And I saw in the midst of the throne and of the four living creatures, and in the midst of the elders, a Lamb standing, as slain, having seven horns and seven eyes, which are the seven Spirits of God [which are] sent into all the earth: and it came and took [it] out of the right hand of Him that sat upon the throne.

And when it took the book, the four living creatures and the twenty-four elders fell before the Lamb, having each a harp and golden bowls full of incenses, which are the prayers of the saints.

And they sing a new song, saying, Thou art worthy to take the book, and to open its seals; because Thou hast been slain, and hast redeemed to God, by Thy blood, out of every tribe, and tongue, and people, and nation, and made them to our God kings and priests; and they shall reign over the earth.

Have you been bought by the blood of Jesus? If so, then you have been made a King and Priest to reign over the earth.

A true king of God reigns over the earth, causing it to flourish! While training and equipping the people for the ministry of reconciliation.

CH.7 NOW THAT WE KNOW THE MESSAGE, LET'S MAKE AN IMPACT!!

In this chapter, we're going to be summarizing what we now know, and I'm going to hopefully help you to translate that into making powerful impact. See, we now know the plan of God. Ephesians 1:9-10 says that at the culmination of the age, all things in Heaven and on earth would come together under the authority of Jesus. Everything coming together under the authority of Jesus, what a glorious day we have to look forward to!

We're going to be talking about <u>imagination</u> quite a bit in this chapter. Our imagination is a gift from God, a superpower that allows us to create from within and manifest it outwardly. Before any house, skyscraper, or business is built it is first conceived in the imagination of someone. But we have to imagine what God wants done, and we have to see it in our heart. I love to do this while lying in bed, after everyone is asleep. I imagine all things on earth and in Heaven coming together!! All things coming under the authority of Jesus, a world with no more evil!!

See this is the whole deal with propaganda is they attack the <u>imagination</u> with false visions and information, so that people will believe for a lie. Once a picture is formed inside of an imagination it becomes part of persons reality, whether it is true or not. Instead, rather **choose to have dominion over your imagination and what you allow in it. Make sure it lines up with the Kingdom Message and the invasion of Heaven's will to earth.**

Use your imagination as a tool to shape and create your future, then the world! The imagination of the heart (a belief or strong desire that can be seen inside) is one of the most powerful forces on the earth. So, we need to make sure that the imaginations of the future we are holding dearly inside of us, are the Truth, The Kingdom Message, and that all of Heaven is coming into this earth. Everything coming under the authority of Jesus Christ, meaning all rulers, all nations, there's no more globalists, no more satanists trying to tell us what to do. These things are fading away as the mountain of the Lord grows.

So, we understand God's purpose for the earth. Reconcile man and reconcile all His creation back to Himself. The issue with false theologies is they get you to imagine something in your heart, and if it's wrong, it's very hard to uproot. You want to hang on to it, because that's your reality, maybe you have even defended it, or preached it. So, meekness and humbleness is required to remove that weed, but God will surely do it if you ask.

Maybe you could say a prayer right now. Something like this, "God, free me from any false beliefs. I am sorry for any false beliefs I have shared, and for any damage that they have caused. Please root them out and fill me with your knowledge of your Will!"

What you see inside of your imagination, whether true or not, is your reality, or what you want to become reality, what you hold dearly inside. So again, <u>we need to make sure we have the correct imagination</u>, and that we also are able ministers to paint the Kingdom picture into the minds and hearts of the believers trapped in "doom and gloom false gospels." Especially those new to the faith.

Romans 8:19-21 **For the creation waits with eager longing for the revealing of the sons of God.** For the creation was subjected to futility, not willingly, but because of him who subjected it, in hope that the creation itself will be set free from its bondage to corruption and obtain the freedom of the glory of the children of God.

Right now, sons of God are manifesting and in this chapter I'm going to teach you about manifesting. How we manifest now that we know we are to rise up and set creation free! Let's make an impact, but what I really mean is let's manifest! As we manifest, creation gets set free.

We don't sit on this knowledge, we don't say, "oh, I need another course" or "I need to go through this five more times." We take this knowledge, we receive it with a good and noble heart, we retain it, and we remember it. It is okay to go through it again. But then we must act, we have to take steps in the right direction to work together to make this world a better place, to rebuild, renew, and restore.

We also must teach the youth, the upcoming generations, because they may soon be the Kingly Royal Families of God that rule the earth!!

You'll be surprised that God does amazing things through us. Especially when we're stepping in harmony with His plan. That's called co-laboring, and most people are walking the other direction because they think things are getting worse and worse. They're in this fight or flight anxiety mode in their minds and building their life accordingly. I've heard one family who got set free from the rapture belief say "We thought the rapture was right around the corner, we were so unmotivated that we got to the point where we didn't even care about making our bed or brushing our teeth because it was the end of the world." And I was like, well, talk about bad fruit.

See without God's vision, people perish. But with His vision people flourish! Get His vision inside of you, get it in your imagination!!

You're supposed to judge a tree by its fruit, or a belief by its fruit. However, believing that all nations shall be blessed, believing that Heaven is invading this earth, and that God's people are rising up bears very good fruit. It even bears real awesome fruit in the physical. As I am writing this at my farm, just about an hour ago I went to the bottom to grab some fruits and came back with some softball sized giant lemons!! We call them Hulk lemons!! Yes, we have those here and I have seen even bigger. I have real fruit because I believe that I am reconciled back to the Garden of Eden.

Alright, we're gonna be talking about the process of manifestation, as a Son or Daughter of God, into a King. Many have heard countless son-ship courses, now it's time for Kingship!

When we understand the plan of God to rebuild, renew, restore, and reconcile the earth, then we

can work with about anyone else who wants to make the world a better place. We can unify and mobilize the masses around this simple thought or question, "How can we work together to make our city a better place, how can we make our world a better place?"

Meditation on these questions brings revolutionary change. Imagine the power of Kingdom Citizens in agreement on these types of things. Maybe you are one of those who will inspire these actions and unity among your city, state, or nation!!!

I want to share a quick story. When I first came to Nicaragua, I came with a ministry. This ministry I came with brought about 40 missionaries every week, and they were from all kinds of different churches. All together in one base, on one bus, in one community, for seven days with a job to build houses.

So, each group got a family, and they built a house for them out of block and wood. We were divided up into teams. Some people did the concrete, some people did the wood, and because we have love in Christ and want to serve, we were able to work together amazingly. We had Church of Christ, Mormons, Baptists, and Pentecostals, all on the same jobs. The guy who was organizing these trips was doing it on purpose, mixing all these churches together. He is a brilliant guy and a great friend who discipled me for around a year. Bless you brother when you read this! I have a lot of love and respect for this man of God and his family.

I learned that when people have a positive Kingdom objective, when people have a destination, when people have a purpose, they can work together for the Kingdom of God with ease.

We see division and competition where there is no purpose and where there there is no clear plan or revelation of God's Will for His creation. Many churches make it about competition rather than collaboration. And that is what we have been seeing for 1000s of years in the body of Christ, a lack of clear purpose. BUT NOW WE HAVE IT!!! The Kingdom Message has been revealed, it's been right under our nose the whole time.

This planet was made for love and righteousness, peace, joy, and harmony. The nature of Jehovah expressed, not the nature of the evil one. We are to manifest the Nature, Power, Divinity, Love, Majesty, and Splendor of Jehovah!

We need to realize this is about teamwork! We have to work together as the Body of Christ, but the only way it's going to happen, in my opinion, is if we have the Kingdom Message. Many need to relearn the Bible for themselves. The Kingdom Message will unify any group of people who have the heart of the Father to make this world a better place for the next generations.

I want to prove that this Kingdom Message you now know, unifies. Here's a question people ask me, "Cory, how do you co-labor with God?" I say, "Well you should ask God these questions," "God, how can I make this world a better place? How can I help to rebuild, renew, and restore the earth? How can I help to bring love? How can I help to bring knowledge? How can I help to bring wisdom into this world? How can I help to bring Heaven? **How can I make this world a better place?**"

These are the questions you ask yourself, you ask your Bible study group, what can we do? God loves to answer these questions. When you guys come up with some ideas, start doing them. Faith is released and Heaven's glory comes to earth, you make an eternal difference. But many people don't do anything, they just talk. You have to take action. Without action your faith is dead. I believe you are an action taker if you have made it this far!

I'm going to give you a bunch of action steps in this chapter. It's not going to be hard. It's going to be fun. It's fun to take action with the Word of God and see supernatural manifestation. I always hope to inspire action when I preach. Why? Because a little bit of faith goes a long way, and if you begin practicing the Word of God you become like the wise man who build his house on the rock! Unshakable!

We now have ourselves in our right mind when we understand the Kingdom Message that is. When we understand that God wants to make this world a better place, and put His people in charge, then we can work together on projects to make that happen all while flowing in harmony with the divine backing and resources from Heaven!

All right. So, to summarize the story of working with all those missionaries... I worked there for about a year, and I didn't see one argument about denomination or theology the whole time. And I was hosting them, hanging out with them, helping them get materials and translate when I could. I never once saw a Baptist arguing with a Mormon, or a Church of Christ with a Pentecostal. They have very different beliefs by the way, and normally they don't connect. **But if you give them a project, they can become best friends.**

What if we all just knew the plan of God instead of accidentally falling into it? This is sure to happen one day soon!

I want to say something here. You may be a part of a denomination. Now I'm not against denominations, I love you all. But we are of the Kingdom not a denomination. The word denomination means to de-nominate. It actually means to remove a person from their positioning to receive a reward. You know, if someone is nominated, they're nominated for an award or to receive a prize.

Denomination is the act of de-nominating someone from a position to receive a reward, look it up. So, it's not a good word and man came up with it.

I am not attacking denominations, but don't become de-nominated from your positioning as a king and son or daughter of God. We are Kingdom Ambassadors. We're building the Kingdom on earth as it is in Heaven, not the biggest denomination. You can enter all these denominations. Just remember don't let man's ideas and doctrines become you, become a King and Priest of God by the blood of Jesus.

So next let's talk about something, I have prospered in business thanks to God. Not like super massively, but I have everything I need for life, and in abundance. Houses, lands, trees, and quite a few animals to establish my family firm in this earth. But before that happened, I had a mentality that was very wrong.

I was a missionary here in Nicaragua, and I thought the way that I was supposed to be a mission work was to receive donations. You preach then say, "Hey, here's my link in the corner, click the link, sow a seed, and here's my vision." I actually did that for around two years. It worked to a degree, but we never really had enough. My family and I were renting the place where we were living and we were struggling financially.

Then one day I remember talking to some missionary friends of mine who were in their 50s, or 60s. They had been missionaries their whole life. I was talking to them one day and said, "Hey, how are you guys doing, how is ministry going?" I was trying to figure out what missionaries are supposed to do to get by financially. Are we supposed to be just receiving donations and live this way our whole life? How does that work? Well, they told me that they're going through some hard times, and they're just trusting in God that their rent money would come. I was like, "oh, no, oh, no, no, God."

I said "God, I don't want to do that when I'm 60, I've been stressing about it for these past two years, I cannot do it that long." Something is wrong. So, from that point on I realized that only receiving donations was not God's best for me. And at that moment I realized that I needed to produce, I needed to build a business or something that would produce wealth for my family and our ministry. But what do I do? I had listened to all the preachers about prosperity, and I tried so much of what they taught to no avail.

I decided one day that I was going to write down a list of business podcasts. I was going to find and listen to people who were actually producing wealth. This to me was a big day because I had only listened to preachers teach on the topic of wealth before, and most of them were not producers. I'm talking about producing products, services, bringing things to the marketplace that people want. Things that help people and make money at the same time. So, I wrote down these podcasts and started listening.

I started learning some things. The first thing I learned was that these wealthy people, some of them were very Godly, and super Kingdom. Like planting millions of trees, feeding millions of families, etc. I listened to a podcast of a billionaire one time, and he said, "If you want to make little impact choose nonprofit, if you want to make big impact, choose for-profit. Because you need profit to run the machine to make more profit to make impact in the world." And I'll say, that's what I had been thinking. I imagine for some people in some situations it may be different.

The other thing I learned was that these high performers were using their <u>imagination</u>, they were using their <u>imagination</u> and talking about it openly. And many of them didn't even know that imagination was their superpower. They would talk about their morning routine and their diet, which I am sure helped, but they were Visionaries, Creators in their Minds.

But that word <u>"Imagination"</u> kept sticking out to me. Then God taught me how to use my imagination to imagine what I wanted in my life. I started planning and thinking about what I really desired to accomplish. I started imagining myself prospering. Then all of a sudden, the idea came to do online marketing. I tried to do it myself which didn't work. I ended up with some interesting questions that led me to find only one guy who could answer one of my questions (showing me he knew what he was talking about). He had a course on online marketing, I took his course, built a business, and it continued to grow from there.

Now, the reason I am saying this is I had a shift of mind. Right before this. I was doing ministry ministry, ministry, nonstop wearing myself out. My family was taken care of financially, but they were number two.

I thought that I had to put the Kingdom first, you know, and then everything would be given. So, my thinking was "His Kingdom first, and then that's how I'll take care of my family the best." But that's not how it works, y'all. You put your family first!! I still preached and taught, but I had to make a decision. And this is not typical advice that you'll probably hear anywhere. I don't know anyone that talks about this; maybe, maybe they do. But I had to make a decision to stop preaching so much, to stop evangelizing so much, and to build my business for a season.

I decided to build this business by faith. That I would establish my family, we would have our own home, our own vehicle, our own land, and that I would work to establish my family firm in the earth. I made that my number one priority. Then after this I would get back to full time preaching.

Well, within about eight months, I built a brand new house which I paid for cash (no loans, no debt). I had all the money for a house, all the money for a car, also a motorcycle, all the things that I wrote on my list, and in eight months!! Why? Because my mission was to establish my family firm in the earth. When I made that my mission I realized, that was God's mission also. And I thought "It's just a house, not a skyscraper, surely I can manifest a house!" And I did, a nice secure beautiful house just like my wife and I wanted! Thanks to God and His blessing! But you gotta believe He is able to do above all we can ask or imagine according to the power that works in us! You gotta take steps, you gotta write it out, declare it, present the plans to God and see it coming to pass, imagining yourself with it.

God needs His Ministers, His Kings, His Apostles, His Prophets, His Teachers, His Preachers, His Evangelists, to be established firm and unshakable in this earth, especially in this time. Kingdom established families will greatly understand rulership.

They will be able to provide Kingdom environments for the growth of new believers, as well as stability and prosperity of whole nations via the blessing of Abraham.

If you love your nation you need to make sure one of these families takes charge! Invite me to speak and declare this message, or even better you speak and declare this message over your nation. All things are possible for those who believe!

We see clearly, now more than ever!! This is good. More good things are coming!

We must realize that our job as Kingdom citizens is to co-labor, co-partner with God and say, "God help me become this oak of righteousness a planting of you to display your splendor. Help me to become unshakable in this earth; give me ideas, show me what to do!!!" Then work on that and realize you may have to take a step back from a few things during this time.

But I'm here to tell you don't get yourself in debt. The opportunity for debt is always there. I'm gonna say something my dad shared with me; he said "If you don't have the money for something, you're not supposed to have it yet, first get the money."

Now I'm not against you if you're in debt, something like 70% of the world is. I'm just saying from now on guys, let's consider this stuff. Because we don't want to be taking on debt from global bankers who are printing this stuff out and playing games with honest people. We're in 2022, where the dollar has a great potential to collapse. And it's unfortunate. Gold and silver coins were used all throughout Bible history, they are a great solution to the upcoming parallel Kingdom economy and Kingdom nations.

So, what do we do? We find out how to get ourselves independent, independent from these systems, independent from the bank debt system, independent from GMO foods, and pharmaceuticals, and all these centralized systems. But once I made this securing of my family and getting free from the globalist systems a priority, God helped me and he helped me very fast, and I never had to stop preaching. Now when I preach, I don't have to ask for donations! I run a Bible Center here in Nicaragua with about 40 families, I haven't asked for donations in a long time, maybe four years, and we're doing bigger things in ministry than ever before.

However, now I feel God speaking to me to lift up a World Wide Kingdom Awake Broadcast Network.

For that I will probably create a larger team and have more serious donations in order to help reach the globe with our broadcasts of the Kingdom Message. I imagine this venture might require a different level of true partnerships; true ministry partnerships are important. Sowing seed is important. However I am not here to teach you that. I am excited though because I know that I can focus ministry seeds now on the projects God gives me.

I don't need donations, I run multiple Kingdom businesses that take care of me and my family. Even if I stopped running those businesses I have already been so blessed. Thank you Father! Glory to you!! Understand me clearly, I am not bragging, I am telling you how you can manifest the same financial freedom in your life too. Then you can do ministry in a powerfully free way, not a slave to your board of directors or those who donate to you. You can do what God has called you to do with people who want to be around you. Not that I am against order, but for me not many people saw the Kingdom Message in the beginning, so God taught me another way of producing for our ministry.

By the way, at the time of writing this, we have successfully been live streaming the Kingdom Message for more than 30 days!! I am in my office right now sitting next to the streaming machine I built, locked and loaded with around 15 Kingdom Messages broadcasting to the new website. Live Kingdom Broadcasting 24/7 would be the goal, with many highly educated and capable Kingdom ministers!!!!

In the beginning of 2020, I started seeing the news about the pandemic. I started seeing all these stimulus packages, so I did the math. I realized they're printing enough money to literally buy almost every piece of property in America. That's how much money they printed and it was a rough estimate. But I realized, oh my gosh, this is a problem. They say that 50% of the currency in USA circulation was printed in the last 18 months to 2 years. So, when I heard that, I said, "Wow, okay, I'm making decent money here, but is this gonna be worth anything in the next five years?" Again, I started thinking differently about wealth. I had to upgrade my thinking once again.

I had this question come to me. It was, "What do I need to do to produce everything I need?" "What do I need to do to produce everything I need?" I wrote a list of everything I use on a daily basis, and I found out that that list wasn't very long. Electricity, water, food, soap, toothpaste, deodorant, check, check, check, check, check them off. Now, of course, we still go out and get a few things. But I have learned how to become independent from these globalist systems. That's what you guys now need to learn as Kingdom citizens with the Kingdom message; how to not be dependent on the systems of the world. Because these systems are incrementally growing worse and worse.

We are called to build better heavenly systems, better heavenly economies, better heavenly cities, everything heavenly and better. This is

quite fun because we are tapping into God's genius!

We must take a step back, and make sure we are not taking the wide road of destruction through convenience, rather than learning what we need to learn and putting it into practice. For example, everyone should have their own private messaging server by now, you can literally set one up in a few clicks. If you need help, holler at me. But this isn't a book on data and privacy, however I could write one. I am just hoping to give you an example here. Take Kingdom! Take Dominion in all areas of life!!! Generate your own solar power, grow your own food, raise your own animals, become your own economy, have many kids to manage it, and so on!!

A lot of the Body of Christ is just plugged on in, plugged on in, and don't want to unplug and come out from behind their screens, well come out!!! The real world is out here! Get some land, get some animals, plant a garden.

See, the enemy wants to impose a false world over humanity, a synthetic world. They want to create a digital world. Why? Well, they don't have dominion in the earth so they create synthetic. When they plant a tree, they get a thorn bush. They want people to put on goggles and live in a digital world. You may think it is cool, but I guarantee the agenda behind it is not; it is to kill off your potential in this earth by putting you into a synthetic domain.

Family, we have to get back to the land, get back to reality. We have to realize we do not need these shiny things, we need each-other, we need God, we need to be working on His Will! Connecting to nature, God, and the Body of Christ! We need to have worship out in nature, which is much more fun!

For a couple of years now I have been hearing in my heart from God *"humanity must get back to the land to go forward."* We must use and build Kingdom infrastructure. It's only a matter of time before the nations realize that we are the only ones qualified to rule on this earth, but we are not waiting around for that. We are building now; many great projects are forming as we speak! We are the only ones who can create stability. The people of God.

You must have the blessing of Abraham, and when you do you can release national blessing!! Every day we get closer to the handing over of the nation's to the people of God. So, get yourself ready, and ask yourself a question, "What can you do to become a producer of something, a product or service of value?" Rather than living as a consumer relying on working a job that for the most part pays fake dollars. What can you do to bring value to the marketplace?

One of the things I did was, I decided to invest in animals, invest in land, plant trees, plant food, save seed. Physical seed is very important to me, it is wealth to me. I can eat what it produces, so can my animals. I can't eat paper money, but I can use it for the things it is used for. See not many people in the Body of Christ are thinking this way, but it is time we elevate our minds to start solving the problems we see, and it is time we start doing it together!! Problem solving can be fun when you use the mind of Christ!

I have a part of my farm that is designated to produce seed from carrots and beets. I have a part in the back of my office that's designated to produce a native type of garlic seed that has probably almost vanished from the face of the earth. It's very awesome and it's native to Nicaragua, but it's very hard to find. I found a guy with a bunch of them, I bought them, and I planted them so I can get a bunch of seed. But how many people do you know thinking about this type of stuff? You can name hundreds of people that consume garlic, right? What about producers? Who of you is saving seed? Who of you is planting flowers for the bees, the butterflies??

I had this question for my son. I said, "son, what would happen if people ate all the carrots on the earth and didn't save any seed. Do you think carrots can disappear off the planet?" Maybe I don't know, but there are plants that I believe have disappeared off the earth because people haven't stewarded the earth correctly. A tomb was found in Egypt that had a vase. It was like 10,000 years old, and there was some seed in it. The seeds were planted and it grew into a plant that was unfamiliar and believed to be currently non-existent on the earth.

We are stewards of the earth, we need to get back to the earth. Not falling for the trap of living in a false digital reality. We need to live in the universe, the reality that God created for us, and soon we will even reach out to the stars. We need to be stewards of this earth; we need to be producers. We need to have Dominion; you need to look for and obtain your land that God has allocated for you. We need to possess the land if the meek are heirs of the earth!

If you know foreigners will work our vineyards and fields, then we need to possess the earth. People say Cory, "You know, you just teach to farm because you farm." NO. I teach to farm because the Bible says the priests of the Lord will have vineyards and animals and lands. Because the Bible said to possess land, I made it my mission to possess land. Now I have some land. Honestly, it has stressed me out sometimes, because it's a lot to clean up and have workers watching animals running around. But I was like, "Thank you, God. I'll figure it out."

I AM figuring it out. And as I'm figuring it out, more keeps coming, and God keeps blessing me. I spent years declaring that I will receive hundreds of houses and hundreds of lands. I spent years declaring that scripture because I left everything to follow Jesus. I have the Blessing of Abraham, and I will manifest these Promises God has given us. I hope you will decide to do so as well!

God is good. God is real. But we need to be believing the Kingdom Message, that we're Kings and we're taking over this planet and **that this earth is ours; we must take possession of it. It's our duty to take possession of it. To increase and to give it to our children, and then teach them the same.**

Get your family secure, build a business, learn skills that bring value to the marketplace and do not live in spiritual La La land. I'm going to explain what that means: waiting for a check in the mail, waiting to win the lottery, waiting for a money miracle. The money miracles do happen. But the real wealth miracle is when you put your hands to the plow, you get an idea, and you manifest it out to the world with perseverance. God blesses the work of our hands.

You know, when I first started my business, I stayed up every night until like three in the morning, woke up at six, studied all day and all night. My wife helped me to do that. We got it done, we didn't give up, we worked together. My first client, boom! Nailed it. Don't give up on your goals. People just need to go a little bit harder at life than what is comfortable. Victory is the only option, make that your mindset.

Now declare "I live life in such extreme victory that I crush evil effortlessly, while enjoying life abundantly!

But you must have your foundation solid, built on the rock. If they come to me and say, "Cory, we're gonna cut your lights off because your speaking too much truth." Haha good luck. I got solar panels everywhere and I doubt you can get past my dogs, or the angels of the Lord. "Cory, we're gonna cut your water off." No, you're not, I got my own well. I also have the Blessing of Abraham (blessed are those who bless me and cursed are those who curse me) so you might not want to try. Are you getting it? Dominion. Kingdom. We work to become independent of their systems.

I don't know if you guys saw this, but they tried this in the USA on quite a few business owners that wouldn't shut down for COVID. The cities were like "We are going to shut off your power, and we will shut off your water if you don't shut down." And they did!! Some of the business owners brought in generators, and some were bringing in water and staying in business.

You see the devils and his minions are little weasels to say it politely. You need to make sure you are ready for the fall of satan's system, it is happening. If there was a "global reset, or collapse" God's people are the ones who will rise up smelling like roses and looking like Glory! Just make sure you do your part to come out from these satanic oppressive systems of control, because the Kingdom of God is manifesting to expose and crush them.

When I saw what those cities did to those business owners, that was proof enough for me to control my own grid and to help others do the same. I have a course called **"Solar Prepped."** So just get yourself and your family out ahead of all this. Become your own economy. Ask God "What can I do to produce and dominate in the wealth arena?" He's probably not going to let you win the lottery, but He's probably going to give you an idea that helps humanity. And then you're going to release that, and you're going to produce wealth.

If you want to learn more, I do have a program called the **"Wealth Mentality Workshop,"** it helps get rid of a lot of sacred cows that believers can have in regarding money. Like, "Oh, that's too much money." No, there's never, never too much. It's only too much when you're thinking about yourself. If you realize what it actually takes to transform whole cities, to grow and influence the right people to make impact, to rebuild whole cities for God, take possession of cities, clean them up, restore them, make them functional, man, there's never too much. We must think outwardly. Jesus said something I want you to meditate on. It is one of the coolest scriptures to get revelation from.

> Luke 11:39-41 Then the Lord said to him, "You Pharisees are so careful to clean the outside of the cup and the dish, but inside you are filthy—full of greed and wickedness! Fools! Didn't God make the inside as well as the outside? **So clean the inside by giving gifts to the poor, and you will be clean all over.**

Most people are trying to clean up themselves by focusing on themselves. Jesus is teaching to look out and work to make the world a better place. You may not be perfect but if you practice this, the righteousness of God will begin to flow through you and make you clean inside, and clean all over! Put first the Kingdom, put first making this world a better place! So much in that tiny passage.

All right, I'm gonna say it one more time, work with God to get yourself and family solid, firm, fixed in the earth and unshakable! Get it!!! Good! Now we can go on!!

Have an unshakable faith that good prevails and that God is working all things together for your good. You know I walked around broke as a joke, didn't have a car, walking around or riding buses in Nicaragua, but declaring "I am prosperous, I have the blessing of Abraham." Two years later it happened. Words have creative power.

Alright, so let's get going through this because I need to teach you something. Now, to establish your family in the earth securely and unshakable, you have to use your <u>imagination.</u> People come to me and they say, "Cory, I'm so frustrated with my life. Nothing's working out. I never have enough time. I say "You're ahead of your imagination." You say what? I say "You're ahead of your imagination, your body is ahead of your imagination, you're a busy body." And usually they say, "Okay, can you explain?" I say, "Yes, you're supposed to sit and meditate and visualize what you want to happen in your day, what you want your life to look like? What do you want your house to look like?" And so on.

How do you want to order your life? You're supposed to imagine your life and whatsoever things you desire to accomplish with the Lord!!! You are supposed to imagine out the completion and the victory of your goals with God.

Imagination is a creative power, and I've proved that in my "**School of Imagination**" *(another powerful resource if you decide to check it out. The resource link will be at the end of the book).* I made this school called "School of Imagination," because God took me into my imagination and showed me how to use it.

I would write a list down of all the things that I wanted to do and imagine them coming to pass, imagine them fulfilled. And I saw the hand of God working with me. So I applied that to ministry, I applied that to my family, I applied that to business, and I started seeing the hand of God moving powerfully in my life.

I believe that because I learned imagination, and how to imagine myself successful, God helped

me to prosper. A lot of people won't imagine. I personally wouldn't use my imagination because I was religious about a certain area. I thought I couldn't imagine what I wanted in life. It's whatever He wants. And that's what most people will say, a lot of people reading this are probably actually in that mind. But I want to encourage you that the Bible says whatsoever things **you desire, when you pray, believe you have received them, and they will be yours. Whatsoever things you desire. Believe you have received them, they'll be yours.**

How do you believe you have received them? You use your imagination, you desire a thing and you imagine yourself receiving it. That's exactly what I'm talking about, and it will be yours. You have a responsibility to learn how to use your Imagination, learn how to see the world becoming brighter and brighter, how to see yourself as the head not the tail, how to see God's plan manifesting not the enemies. So, if there were a part two to this book, I would say take the **"School Of Imagination"** it will help tremendously in unlocking the power of your imagination so you can begin creating the future you desire.

There are so many people that halfway start millions of things. Don't do that. Find out what you want. Take an extra day to think about it. What do you really want and why? Why do you want that house, why do you want five houses? Draw it out of your heart and then make it happen. You have to make it happen. But God works through you. He blesses the work of your hands; He starts giving you ideas. What do you want?!! God's asking us "whatsoever things do you desire." You have freedom in Christ. God is not micromanaging everyone. He's a Father not a slave-driver. There are countless directions you could go to reach your destination, decide, and commit. Bring it before the Lord, bring your blueprints to Him in your prayer session.

People think that there's only one way I have to go in this life, and I have to wait for God. When in reality you're supposed to be using your imagination. We already know the plan, make the world a better place, and take over the earth for Jesus, simple. Now how do you desire to make that happen? What skills do you have or could you obtain?

I give my son freedom to imagine the future he wants, and I'll help him with it. Do you think God is different? Ask yourself, what do you want? People have never asked themselves that because they have said, "It's whatever you want God," and they keep pushing it off to Him like that's the right thing to do. I did this. I learned this life tip the very hard way. God taught me this and if we had more time, I would explain more. But that's for another day. So just pray about this one! We will speak more on this in the future hopefully.

As a next step, go through my **"School of Imagination."** Apply these things, apply what you're learning here. Get your family established firm. Then begin looking out to the world, at your community, and ask, "What can I do that will produce a lasting impact, lasting fruit?" We are here to produce fruit that lasts." (John 15)

See, we must get the personal victory for us and our families. Then the NEXT STEP is we begin to look out and focus the power of the Blessing towards our community and the nations and begin praying for them. While you are working on your personal victory, begin to look out to the nations and pray for Heaven's invasion! Praying for Heaven's invasion, and the blessing of all nations, is one terrific way of keeping first the Kingdom of God.

What God really needs is He needs a bunch of His Children to be firm in this earth, not dependent on these globalist centralized systems. He needs His people to be producers of wealth, in one accord, of one mind and understanding, working together to manifest His Will!

Once these personal victories happen, the Body of Christ has to get to a place where there are established families, that are a testimony of the Kingdom of God and its Blessing. These families must get together, and they must operate as the Kings of the Earth. They also must start projecting into the future what we want this planet to look like for our children. We have been leaving that up to the wrong group of people, again because the Church has believed it's the end of the world. Well good news flash, IT IS NOT THE END OF THE WORLD!!

I prophesy that soon Royal Kingdom Families will emerge as Rulers of this earth!

This is a big deal. Now I want to explain something. Obviously in the year 2022-2023 we have an issue with these devil worshiping globalists and mad scientists, who want to depopulate the planet. They want to do and launch all this crazy stuff. They have a problem. They have a problem and they are possessed with these evil spirits, **but we are the solution.**

Things are changing. They can't hide anymore. They are being exposed and soon they will be brought to justice.

These satanists have spent decades creating all kinds of documents projecting the future they want for the inhabitants of the planet, and they don't even know God. They have a document called "The future we want." They want smart sensors in everything. The ability to read everyone's emotions, everyone's thoughts, read, write thoughts into your mind, execute commands in your mind. They want complete control of human biology. That's the future they want. They want to actually merge with machines and make humanity follow along.

We need to talk about real issues as the Body of Christ. For too long the Church has been like "Let's just ignore the elephant in the room, let's just ignore the devil governor." We have the power to fix these issues Kingdom Family! Where are the Church's documents of the future we want????

God gave this earth to us. Are we gonna take it back or what!! Where is our unity and our hope for a brighter future WITH GOD IN IT! Where is our projection of the future? Where is our plan and declaration for the world to read? Do you get what I'm saying?? Let's make one!!

God showed us all things in Heaven and on earth coming under the authority of Christ Jesus but guess what? He didn't give us a blueprint. He gave this earth to man. That's why we have to come up with solutions, just like you have to come up with solutions for your personal life. You have to imagine what you want in life and make it happen. But once we get the personal victory, we transition to the nation level. You could call it the Ecclesia where we gather as the Body of Christ, and WE decide and agree on a future we want, for our state, our nations, our world. But we need to be discussing what we will allow and what we won't allow into the future.

We as the sons and daughters of God are the most powerful creations on this planet, not the sons of satan. We need to put our agenda out there. We need to come up with Kingdom Heavenly solutions for the school systems, for the medical systems, for the money systems, for the technology systems, regulations and limits on how far we go with certain things like AI (artificial intelligence). The people working on AI know it is a bad idea and they should be stopped. There's a race and competition to make the best AI that will control the most data and be the best and fastest, because they're not regulating it.

There are some lines that should have already been drawn in the sand, and they need to be drawn by the kings of God stating, "We will not do this or that in our country." Who is qualified to say things like this, according to God? Only the people of God, the communities of the people of God! The gatekeepers of God!

I'm not trying to freak you out, we are definitely not hopeless here, but do you guys even know about smart cities, what they're attempting? What these different companies are trying to do? They're approaching **mayors** all over the world to get signed agreements to build smart cities, to put smart sensors in everything to read, write, execute commands, even issue ownership of the people's biology.

The mayors... Get it? "Authority over cities," it starts at the city level. Talk to your mayors, become a mayor if you decide. Do not sit back and let your mayor remain uneducated to this demonic garbage in the name of Jesus.

Smart cities are a massive invasion of our biology, smart phones as well, and I guarantee that many of these mayors have no idea about any of this dark technology. I did a podcast on smart cities (Kingdom Business Lifestyle Podcast), you should download it personally and share it with your mayor. Isn't that a line in the sand Church??! Or do you all want smart sensors reading your biology, your thought life, and modifying your emotions? We must wake up and say no. Having and using smart devices is not smart anymore. Especially when each one has the potential to become a weapon against the user, even a literal electromagnetic weapon in many cases! **We must go back to go forward.**

We need to decide as the body of Christ, do we want that stuff or not? And we shouldn't!! We need to talk about this stuff as Kings and Government officials, not just sitting in our pews hoping Jesus returns and saves us from this mess. We need to agree, pray, and make it happen. Remember we are the most powerful group on the planet. We just need to realize it! So let's agree to make this world a better place, and possess the leadership of the nations in Jesus name!

So, what should happen now that we have the Kingdom Message? Well of course rule number one, we should be working to establish our family! Working to build businesses of value, produce wealth, possess the earth, but also getting together with others who understand this and using the authority we have inside to transform the future. We should look into the future and see a world that we want as Heaven invades, and make it known!! We need to imagine and manifest the world with abundance, a world where the people carrying the wisdom of God are the only leaders.

I know people can plant a garden. What does the future look like when we train kids in agriculture, in permaculture? What if the youth all started learning about gardens, abundance, ruler-ship, and the truth that we are reconciled back to God through Christ.?

In the beginning of this Kingdom transition into power, there are ideas like this, but they have to be implemented. The people of God need to be using their voices in these school boards, we need to be owning schools. In these town halls, we need to not only speak there, but we also need to be the leaders and organizers. We need the Body of Christ to start using the Mind of Christ and begin thinking much bigger!

We don't have to force our agenda on people, but we do need to make the Kingdom agenda of God known!! Our agenda is not a controlling agenda. It's a liberating agenda, an educating agenda, a freedom and liberty plan. See the globalists want to depopulate and dumb down humanity, but we want to populate and educate and reach the stars.

There is so much God has created for us, and we have so much more power to rise up into it. Again, we in Christ are the most powerful beings on the earth. Let us now come together. We must stop being religious like the pharisees. We have to stop being in competition and start putting the objectives in front of us, with clear simple goals. We need to start being leaders and have Bible study groups teaching the simple Kingdom Message, Heaven on earth. We need to start listening to real Kingdom Preachers not politically correct yes men. It's the knowledge of truth that makes us free. Never underestimate the power of any sized Bible study group!

So, I know this chapter may seem heavy to some, but these are my ideas of manifestation. You can take what blesses you and apply it and throw away what doesn't. You may have other ideas of how we manifest as sons and daughters of God and take Dominion making this world a better place. Talk about them! We all need to get to this place where we're discussing what the future looks like as we enter our Kingship positions. Are we going to believe the Bible or not?

The Bible says that God swore by His own self, all nations would be blessed. Jesus even flipped over the tables and said, "My house will be called a house of prayer for all nations." We're supposed to be praying for the nations to be blessed, for God's people to take over! Can you see it yet!? If so, shout to me in the Spirit a big AMEN!

And if we start talking about these things, guess what? The whole narrative changes. That's a whole bunch of faith to start talking about the future where God's people are in charge! But I'm here to tell you all, we have a whole bunch of people who have Holy Ghost power, and they don't know how to use it.

They have this Holy Ghost, powerful weapon, if you will. But their mind doesn't allow the Holy Spirit to flow freely. Their mind has strongholds, they have religion, and they think that the world's getting darker and darker. To believe that and to speak that over your kids!? Imagine the kids how they feel growing up being taught that things are going to get worse and worse. They grow up without any hope. That's the worst type of life to live; a life without hope. I lived it. We must change this and empower the youth!!

But now I have great hope. God came to give us a future, to give us a hope. So do as much as you can to get this Kingdom Message out. We're keeping it short and sweet and with depth at the same time so that you can grab this book, you can teach or talk about this in a study group and then say, "Hey guys we have the power, who wants to be mayor? Who wants to be attorney general? Who's qualified?" Find some people in your area, get them together. Talk about the Kingdom Message and go bless, teach, and free creation. Creation is waiting to see what you will do!!! No pressure!

One more important note: If God has allowed you to see something, that is because you have the power to do something.

Did you know people can be voted into leadership positions of all sizes by just a small study group? Voted into a throne by a Bible study group. We should have been doing this a long time ago. But it's okay. Now's the time, no more evil in the high places in Jesus' name!

I hope that this book inspires you. I believe that you now have the Kingdom Message taking root into your heart!!! Make sure you also have the audio edition of this book preserved for the future. Faith comes by hearing and this is a message that you can greatly reap from hearing over and over!

Preserve this physical book as well for the future generations. We are not going to lose, or have hidden, our Kingdom history and heritage anymore!

Remember we are Born Again from Heaven, and by the blood of Jesus, we have been made Kings and Priests that reign over this earth. We have an

inheritance from God and part of that inheritance is this earth.

This earth is ours in Christ!!! It is our duty to imagine the future. We as the Kings of God are to corporately connect and imagine the future we desire and then we make it happen with the help of God!

I'm gonna say that one more time, it is our duty to imagine the future. We as the Kings of God are to corporately connect and imagine the future we desire and then we make it happen with the help of God!

If we don't, as the body of Christ, project for the masses the future of the Kingdom of God, then there is a void. And these evil doers have been projecting into that void. Let's shut it down and redirect eyeballs to the Kingdom Message, the will of the Father, Heaven on earth!

God's plan in His heart was always to make us into a Holy Nation, a Holy Kingdom Nation high above the nations of the earth. The positions of supreme power are for the people of God, and that's what this generation is stepping into now!! I'm excited to be going there with you all. Thank you so much for reading. I'll see you in the next one!

Deuteronomy 28:1 "And it shall come to pass, if thou shalt hearken diligently unto the voice of Jehovah thy God, t**o take heed to do all His commandments which I command thee this day, that Jehovah thy God will set thee supreme above all nations of the earth**"

1 Peter 2:9-10 But *ye* [are] <u>a chosen race, a kingly priesthood, a holy nation,</u> a people for a possession, that ye might set forth the excellencies of him who has called you out of darkness to his wonderful light; who once [were] not a people, but now God's people; who were not enjoying mercy, but now have found mercy.

Now Go Forth Holy Royal Nation Of Kings And Priests!! It's Time To Rule And Reign!!

This book is written in honor of my lovely wife Kimberly Gray, and my awesome son Asher Ezekiel Gray. Thanks for continuing to love and believe in me and the Jesus in me!!! Love you guys!

Connect more and find additional resources at:
https://kingdombusinesslifestyle.com

Manufactured by Amazon.ca
Bolton, ON

32426422R00162